To Jeanne
my friend
neighbor!
Warm wishes!
Nora
4-20-00

M. Nora McGlashan

O DAYS OF

M. Nona McGlashan
Illustrated by Patricia Houk

WIND
& MOON

FITHIAN PRESS, SANTA BARBARA, 1997

Copyright © 1997 by M. Nona McGlashan
All rights reserved
Printed in the United States of America

Published by Fithian Press
A division of Daniel and Daniel, Publishers, Inc.
Post Office Box 1525
Santa Barbara, CA 93102

Book design: Eric Larson

LIBRARY OF CONGRESS CATALOGING-IN-PUBLICATION DATA
McGlashan, M. Nona
    O days of wind and moon / by M. Nona McGlashan
      p. cm.
    ISBN 1-56474-232-6 (alk. paper)
    1. McGlashan, M. Nona. 2. Wei, Candida. 3. Sisters of Social Service—China—Shanghai—Biography. 4. China—History—Civil War, 1945–1959—Personal narratives, American.   I. Title.
BX4705.M4762A3   1997
266'.2'092—dc21
[B]   97-11702
                                                         CIP

In memory of
sister Candida Wei, SSS

My valiant partner in this venture, she was the first to dream of a Chinese branch of the Sisters of Social Service, later established at Taipei, Taiwan.

Contents

Introduction 11

China Bound, 1946 15

We Arrive at Shanghai and Settle In 20

A Taste of Shanghai Social Life 27

We Are on Our Own and Work Begins 32

Letters Home, 1947 38

Fieldwork for My Students 50

The Russian Connection 55

Jeep Adventures 60

Where Can I Find a Rest Room? 69

Moon Festival Time—
    We Move Into Our Own Home 72

The Russian Disconnection 79

What to Do About Lillian? 83

1947 Draws to a Close 88

1948 Begins 95

A Change in the Wind 99

Waning of the Moon 104

What Happened After 111

APPENDIX: An Historical Perspective 113

Sister Alice

Sister Candida Wei

Sisters Candida and Magdolna

*Clockwise from upper left:
Sisters Mariel, Lucile,
Magdolna, Candida,
and Alice
Shanghai, 1948*

Sister Lucile

Sister Mariel

Sister Malia

Introduction

Years have passed since I returned to secular life after twenty years as a Catholic Sister of Social Service. From a store of treasured memories of that time, this book is about the twenty-three months I spent in China. In 1946 Sister Candida Wei and I were sent to Shanghai to lay the groundwork for a Chinese branch of our Society. Our expected reinforcements were delayed for more than a year by political upheavals in the aftermath of World War II.

My most vivid personal experience lay within the framework of that first year of discoveries, decisions, trials and errors. With the breakdown of my own health I had to return home before the others.

I offer this memoir for what it is, no more no less, a recollection of how it was and how it seemed to me. If it fills in a small segment of the total picture of China before the old gave way to the new and present regime, I am glad. But I have not tried to give it more significance than it deserves.

I have changed the Chinese names of my students and friends in order to preserve their privacy. After fifty years, my memory of Chinese characters and spoken language has long since deserted me, so I have not tried to use this method of conjuring up a show of authenticity when, after all, it is not necessary.

One of the most famous couplets in Chinese Zen literature reads:

An eternity of endless space:
A day of wind and moon.

The poem is open to endless speculation as to its meaning, but even without interpretation, the second line is so Chinese it seemed a metaphor of my China experience. I couldn't resist it for a title.

My affinity for China and all things Chinese began in early childhood. I was adopted and raised by my grandparents, Charles and Leonora McGlashan of Truckee, California. An attorney, my grandfather frequently took us on his business trips to San Francisco. Besides visiting relatives, these trips always included a fascinating stroll through Chinatown. On my fourth birthday my most wonderful gift was a blue silk kimono with green and lavender butterflies, matching slippers and a perfumed folding fan. I think from that day, I was China-bound.

After the death of my grandparents I became a Catholic and, in 1936, entered the Sisters of Social Service, at that time a radically modern society. Founded in Budapest, Hungary, the American foundation was in Los Angeles, California. For the next ten years, I worked mainly among the Italians, Hispanics and Blacks of the inner city. The families of these small run-down homes and vermin-infected apartments became my own. Much of my service entailed linking particular need with the appropriate agency. Most of my work, however, was with the hundreds of children who spilled into our afterschool clubs and classes. We gathered in a large gymnasium attached to the small mission church. In the evening we met with teenagers. With athletic equipment and supervised dances, we succeeded in transforming young gangsters into proud members of the community.

At the time that I entered the Sisters of Social Service, my only request was that I be sent to China, if ever we made a foundation there. And so it came to pass. This book is the account of my "days of wind and moon."

Many have helped me write this memoir. My first thanks go to the Sisters of Social Service at Los Angeles for permission to print letters we wrote from China and for graciously granting access to other material from their archives. Special thanks to Sisters who read the final draft critically and otherwise encouraged and helped me. I am indebted to Sister Jean Marie Renfro, S.S.S., who was in charge of the archives before her untimely death. I particularly thank Sisters Beneta Nolan and Stephana O'Leary for approving the typescript and otherwise facilitating completion of the memoir.

That I undertook to write about those China years is largely due to the prodding of my cousin, Betty H. McGlashan, a retired history and English teacher. We were both in China about the same time without knowing it. Married to the district traffic manager for Pan American World Airways, she boarded the last plane to leave China and from high above saw Mao's armies marching toward Shanghai. Thanks, Betty, for thirty years of nudging, also for reading and editing.

I am indebted to Florence Turner, Ph.D., for many years a teacher of Asian studies and expert in Chinese civilization, for clarifying for me what Mao was doing while I was in Shanghai. I needed that substantial reality to give my story perspective.

The Auburn Library reference help was very important to me and graciously given. I am indebted to David Gilmore, cousin and a library volunteer, for cheerfully getting and returning needed books as well as for his unfailing support.

Since I am legally blind, I owe thanks to many who read to me and helped with revisions and corrections. Of these, Rosie Stilwell, Joan Bakotich, Jeanie Graham and Minnie Clark gave unforgettable assistance.

Another I must thank for encouraging me on to the finish line is Persia Woolley, a friend and prolific Auburn writer.

From 1946–49, Fenton (Brad) Bradley, RMC USN, was

assistant Navy director of the Port of Shanghai. From his office overlooking the harbor, he witnessed the parades to the execution grounds. I thank him for sharing this memory. I also thank Brad for the many times I have drawn on his knowledge and perspective as the historian and teacher he became before his retirement.

I also thank Tom Barr, who gave of his computer expertise in typing the background history in the addendum.

Above all, I thank Rita Cloutier, friend and typist, who mastered the computer for the book's sake and mine. A former reporter, she was of enormous help to me as I groped for a vocabulary in oral speech. As a writer, I have always drawn on language that seemed to come from a different filing cabinet than the one I used in spoken utterance.

My gratitude goes equally to my nephew, Robert N. (Bob) Rogers, Ph.D., who gave unstintingly of vacation time to reading, editing and computerizing the manuscript. He also recorded the completed manuscript on tape, enabling me to make corrections and revisions.

Finally, I am eternally grateful to my recently deceased cousin, Naida Gilmore Palmer, whose unfailing support continues to encourage me on.

—1—

China Bound, 1946

Every lifetime needs at least one golden moment of dreams come true. Mine came to me that October night of 1946 when from the top deck of the SS *Marine Lynx* I followed my superior, Sister Frederica Horvath, down the steep narrow stairway to the Shanghai wharf and good earth of China. Close behind came Sister Candida Wei, my partner in this China venture. I could hear her excited little laugh, mingled with sobs, and knew her thin face was wet with uncontrollable tears of homecoming joy. Nine years and a world war had intervened since she had seen the brothers and sister waiting for her on the dock. For me, too, it seemed a homecoming, for I had long ago adopted China in my heart.

When we reached the bottom of the stairway, Candida was immediately caught up in her family's loving embrace. Bouquets of red roses were pressed into Sister Frederica's arms and my own. The rest became a swirl of impressions, excited chatter that was unintelligible to us for language but perfectly understood for emotion. Magically, Frederica, Candida and I were riding in the Wei family's chauffeured limousine through the wide business streets of Shanghai. Vividly I remember the darkness of that mid-October night. It must have been moonless. The hour was probably nine-thirty. We moved slowly, with incessant honking of our car horn and everyone else's. Only headlights illumined the street. I clearly recall there were no street lights or lamps along our way.

In the headlights we saw bicycles dart in and out of the traffic lanes. Tall traffic signals loomed before us, with platforms large enough for a traffic cop to manipulate the red stop light which shone like a ruby in the darkness. Clearly I remember a Chinese soldier standing beneath the platform holding a bayonetted rifle. The war was over so I mentioned this soldier. I learned he was a policeman. With a bayonet? A rifle? Yes, call the police if you are being robbed, and they will drive away the robber and rob you themselves, I was told. This was a jarring note to the dream of arrival.

• • •

Soon after World War II ended in August 1945, Sister Frederica realized she had a problem. As superior of the Sisters of Social Service at Los Angeles, how was she to tell Candida, her diminutive Chinese sister, there would be further delay in her return to her homeland? Now that communication lines were open between the USA and China, this Shanghai-born sister was certain she would soon join her family. For that purpose she had come to us in 1938.

But organizations don't or can't move that fast. For one thing, the Los Angeles branch of the Sisters of Social Service was small. It was the only American branch of this organization, founded and headquartered in Budapest, Hungary. Not only did Sister Frederica lack sisters to spare for a new foundation, but communication with the Motherhouse and our top superior had only just reopened. Red tape and protocol would do nothing to hurry things along. Then there was the necessary invitation from the Bishop of Shanghai to warrant our moving to his diocese.

The small number in the Los Angeles house gave us a warm feeling of family. Breakfast was the meal when we were all together around the long table, for most of us brown-bagged our lunches to eat at youth centers or agencies. If we had evening meetings, we brown-bagged that meal as well. Across the breakfast table we rejoiced with our little Chinese sister when her dream of going home seemed assured. And again across that table, we knew her disappointment when told of further delay, especially since her first letter from home had announced her father's death.

Born in Shanghai October 15, 1910, she was the second girl child in the family. As such, she was not scheduled to live. However, her mother's death followed the birth within a few days. By the time attention could be paid to the baby, she had charmed the brothers and sister with her happy disposition. They called her "Apricot Smile." And her father agreed that the baby should live. She was to become his favorite. After graduating from Morning Star, a Catholic middle school, she expressed a desire to join the Catholic Church. It had been her father who told her to follow her heart. When she was baptized she chose Gladys for her Christian name as a near translation of "smile."

And in 1936, when she learned of the unusual religious community that worked directly with the people, he alone of all the family did not oppose her continuing to follow her heart. Her first attempt to leave China was thwarted when her brother John bodily removed her and her luggage from the ship bound for America. She finally made it in 1938, this time by plane.

Member of a wealthy family, she had astonished her friends and relatives by her concern for the poor. The general attitude was fatalistic. Karma explained the beggar's life to most people of eastern religious persuasion. She learned of the work of the Sisters of Social Service, who wore uniforms, not traditional habits, allowing freedom of movement for driving cars and supervising camping trips for underprivileged youngsters. This was for her. To be close to the poor, sharing their struggles and tears, to work with children who otherwise ran the streets, this too was for her. In her application to the Society, she specified that she wanted to bring the community back to her own country as a Sister of Social Service.

By odd coincidence, shortly after her application to the SSS I, too, applied. And I, too, specified that I would like to be sent to China if and when a foundation were started. There were other parallels between us. Born on opposite sides of the Pacific, we were both twenty-five, converts to Roman Catholicism with strong religious calling. At the same time, we each desired to join the SSS and bring it and its work to China.

For all that year following war's end, Sister Frederica waited out the slow communication between her own top superior in Hungary and the almost total silence from the bishops in China. In her last communiqué the Superior General told her she had appointed Sister Alice, a Hungarian, to head the China foundation. It would take time to disengage her from present responsibilities. Finally, a letter from the Bishop of Shanghai gave permission to start a house in his diocese. He made it clear this was not an invitation imposing on him an obligation to provide housing.

Meanwhile Sister Candida carried on her work at the Chinese Center. She grew paler and thinner. By no word or action did she express the deep sadness this prolonged exile caused. But we all guessed it, and no one more than our Superior, who had been and still was, to an extent, cut off from her own motherland, Hungary.

Sister Frederica had dashed Candida's hopes for a quick return to China, at the same time giving assurance of future action. But the dashing of hopes was too much for the word "future" to heal. Candida became deathly ill, and Sister Frederica decided to act on her own initiative.

I remember it was a warm summer afternoon in 1946 when I came home early from my youth center and was told that Sister Frederica wanted me in her office.

"Sit down, Sister Mariel," she said, her soft voice with its strong Hungarian inflection serious, but with a smile. I was totally unprepared for her next words, which came straight to the point.

"I want you to get your passport, Sister." She smiled broadly at the amazement in my face. "You will go to China with Sister Candida. We must all get shots, for I will go with you and stay until you are settled. You will be acting Superior until the Hungarian sisters join you."

Stunned, speechless, this was heart-stopping news. I should have thought, at least, why me when there are others more experienced, more qualified. No such thought entered my head. My faith told me and all my religious training told me, when your Superior sends you, God sends you. You just go.

Candida turned over her work among the Asian population to another sister, as I did mine, and we quickly found ourselves at the very door of departure. I remember the bubonic plague shot hurt the most. The aching moan of my arm chanted thrillingly, going to China, going to China....

~2~

We Arrive at Shanghai and Settle In

We were to sail on the SS *Marine Lynx*, a converted troop ship, leaving San Francisco on September 29th. After a gala bon voyage dinner the night before, the three of us took the Southern Pacific train from Los Angeles to Oakland, where we spent the night with sisters in our Oakland settlement house. Next day we were joined by sisters from the Sacramento house. Thus, we were escorted to the ship by an impressive showing of gray uniforms and veils.

After watching trunks and luggage being lowered into the hold and exploring the ship from one end to the other, our sisters gave us final hugs and good wishes. We saw them waving at the three of us as, at long last, we got under way and headed through the Golden Gate.

On board were four hundred returning missionaries of all denominations. Nuns returning to Philippine missions neighbored our cabins and regaled us with tales of experiences before the war. They were happy to be going back to the people they served and loved.

The Superior amused us with a story that warned me of a particular hardship of missionary life—the scarcity of rest rooms. Natives of some cultures don't comprehend our desire for privacy in such matters. When once before this nun had been away from the mission on sick leave, the Filipinos had welcomed her back with songs and dances by the chil-

We Arrive at Shanghai and Settle In

dren. Then, they ceremoniously presented her with a gift. Two lads entered with a flower-wreathed chamber pot, suspended on a pole they carried between them on their shoulders. This was considered very special and something only a foreigner would value. They set it down before her with the greatest respect.

A Jesuit priest and four seminarians were aboard. They would study Mandarin at the Peking University and be assigned to a mission.

Two Anglican nuns, dressed in traditional nuns' garb but wearing crosses, not crucifixes, looked more Catholic than we did in our gray uniforms and berets. We abandoned the hat and veil, which would have doubtless blown out to sea on the wind. A reporter in his paper printed a large picture of us aboard the ship the first day, calling us Episcopalian deaconesses, which we probably did resemble.

We were sixteen days on the Pacific. I remember the night I looked up at the star-filled sky and said, "Look, Sister, we are in the Orient." I cannot describe the subtle change, but the sky, the stars, the night were Oriental.

In the early dawn of October 15 a sudden change in the throb of the ship's engine brought me out of bed to peer through the porthole of my cabin. Sure enough. While we slept, the SS *Marine Lynx* had slipped into the Shanghai harbor. Sampans, bulky junks, fishing boats and other vessels I had seen only in pictures busily plied the waters. Near us, trim steamers flew colors of various nations.

I hurriedly dressed, bent on joining Sisters Frederica and Candida. I found them beginning to pack, so back to my own cabin I scurried to follow suit. Hurrying through the narrow passageways I heard no sound of voices. I knew my fellow passengers were preoccupied as I was, with thoughts and hopes for new beginnings.

All day long, without food or drink (a lack we ignored, so intense was our excitement) the three of us stood on the top deck around the rail, gazing down at the crowded wharf. In a cluster, Candida's family sat on boxes or stood throughout the day, waving to her from time to time in response to her own thrown kisses and communicative gestures.

Sister Frederica and I stood on either side of Candida, joining her in waving and smiling down at her family's upturned faces. We hardly spoke among ourselves. I knew that my Superior, foundress of the American community and about to found the China house, was absorbed in her memories and thoughts.

Darkness gathered, obscuring our view. At eight o'clock strong searching beams were trained on the ship from top deck to bottom and the passengers' silence broke with a universal sigh of relief. From the lower deck, they swarmed quickly onto the wharf. A narrow stairway was quickly raised from the wharf to where we stood on the top deck. Removal of a segment of rail formed a gateway for our descent.

• • •

We were to lodge with the Mesdames of the Sacred Heart who owned and administered Aurora Women's College in the heart of Shanghai. The large, attractive Western-style red brick building occupied almost a city block. The convent adjoined the college. The Japanese had used the entire compound to intern missionary prisoners.

We were warmly welcomed by this British congregation. My only sharp memory is of the coffee. We had not eaten since the night before but now I remembered coffee. It was my only request, although I am sure we were served a substantial repast with it. To my dismay they brought café au lait, of a very light brown shade. As politely as I could, I asked if I might have straight black coffee and wondered at the disbelieving glances and words like, "Are you sure?" When I said yes, I was sure, off went a slim little Chinese novice to the kitchen. She returned with a thick, blackish brew and I understood two things. One, this was another country with other habits; and two, I had best get used to their ways fast.

Sister Candida and I shared a neat, white cubicle of a room with twin beds, table and two chairs. This would be our home until we could find and finance (with help, we hoped, from home) a convent of our own. Sister Frederica was shown to a room which she would occupy until she had us settled and prepared to fly on our own. It would take about two months. The sisters back home wanted her home for Christmas and this was the middle of October, time enough to do a lot, if you were a Sister of Social Service.

We went down a flight of stairs next morning to breakfast in an austere room with concrete walls like those of our upstairs sleeping rooms. But a long dining table was already filling with missionary nuns of other orders and happy, informal chatter prevailed. We were introduced or introduced ourselves, found seats among the other guests and were quickly served the beverage of choice (yes, café au lait again) if you didn't want tea. A plate of golden scrambled eggs slid magically before each hungry diner.

Some of the nuns were newly arrived from Hong Kong or had fled the Communists from missions in the interior. Others had never left China and told harrowing incidents of internment right here at Aurora during Japanese occupation.

We would often find new faces and the religious garb of yet another order of nuns, for the Sacred Heart sisters hospitably welcomed all who were either arriving or just passing through. Some were new arrivals from the States or other countries, but more were refugees from the interior, whose missions were threatened by the growing civil war. Where they were bound for we didn't know. They themselves were waiting for directions from their Superiors, whether to locate elsewhere or return to home countries. The nuns we met were, for the most part, from Europe.

Maryknollers, of course, were American. English was the spoken language at these meals, whatever the nationality of the sister.

From these refugees we began to learn how harshly Communists were treating Christians and clergy. They told of an elderly bishop who had been forced to stand on a table while his Christian parishioners jeered and then threw the table over. I believe he broke his hand or some fingers. Incidents such as this alarmed us, but we still did not really realize how extensive the distant warfare would become. Sister Frederica enjoyed meeting Hungarian nuns and clergy stopping over in Shanghai from the interior. I recall meeting Spanish, Italian, Belgian, French, Dutch, Polish, German and Hungarian sisters at the pleasant morning gatherings.

Sister Candida was picked up by her brother's chauffeur almost immediately after breakfast and went with him to spend the week with her family.

Sister Frederica and I explored Shanghai by foot, bus and pedicab. On leaving the college we passed the red brick gatekeeper's cubicle where Lau Papa sat holding a glass of hot tea. He was very thin and wrinkled, with long strands of gray beard on each side of his thin lips. It was his job to check who came in and out of the campus entrance. He had great dignity and importance in the eyes of all.

Before all else, we paid a formal call on the kindly French Bishop of Shanghai at Zi-Ka-Wei. In addition to the bishop's residence and offices, this section of Shanghai was noted for the Catholic girls school, Morning Star, run by the Helpers of the Holy Souls. The bishop received us cordially, explaining why he had not felt free to invite us to his diocese. Not only were resources and repairs from war and occupation a consideration, but he was not sure of the future. A year or two would tell the tale, he thought, alluding to the civil war now disrupting the interior. But he welcomed our mission as a new and needed approach to people's problems in China. It was understood we would be responsible to find our own lodging.

The bishop's reference to a civil war in the interior passed over my head like a summer breeze. I had no way of knowing any more political facts than that the country was divided between the Communists and Chiang Kai-shek's forces, or Nationalists. I did not know that only the year before, in the spring of 1945, more than a million Chinese Communists had held a Congress at Yenan, establishing Mao Tse Tung as Chairman and leader of the CCP (Chinese Communist Party). Mao had proposed a coalition government with the Nationalists, and Chiang Kai-shek appeared to concur. After months of negotiations, neither the CCP nor Chiang's government seemed to accept what coalition really meant (who would head it) and talks broke down. The civil war began again in earnest in late June 1946. Nationalist armies began the offensive in the Central Plains.

From Zi-Ka-Wei, Sister Frederica and I took a pedicab back to the main streets of town. I could not get over the beauty of colors I saw in the parks and gardens of the city and outside the city, in the green landscape. Green was so much greener, blue sky so much bluer than at home in the USA. No smoke from industry veiled the atmosphere. I wondered why I had never heard or read of this natural beauty of China. When I saw for the first time a little mill being turned by a water buffalo patiently treading around and around in a circle, I felt I had been transported back in time. Riding in a *ricksha* at the pace a man could walk gave time to think, to look, to observe. I wondered at our Western time-is-money rush to the exclusion of thinking and of dreaming.

I thought the city itself was beautiful. However, I was not prepared for it to look so Caucasian. International city that it was, the plenitude of firms, banks and even department stores of British, French, German or other European origin left only the Chinese characters on billboards and advertisements to assure me I was in China.

Unexpected, too, were the crowds of people overflowing from sidewalk to roadway in the downtown commercial area. Here the majority of merchants and businessmen wore the modern version of the mandarin gown, a long, unbelted garment with wide sleeves. Our ricksha coolies, on the other hand, wore short jackets and trousers. I was told that the city's population had swollen to three million within a few months. Refugees from the interior were still arriving, and not all were Chinese. From Harbin in the north, the White Russians (not Soviet) had fled the advance of Mao Tse Tung's Communist troops. Shanghai was a logical destination for them since jobs were possible, if not plentiful.

The city had either not been badly damaged by bombs or had repaired damage rapidly, for we saw none. We did see a factory or two with machinery at a standstill, waiting for power to run it. Around the factory were vacant cabins for workers and their families. Electricity was still rationed throughout the city. The college area where we were staying had lights for only a specified hour or two each night. We purchased oil lamps, remembering what spoiled Americans we were, and enjoyed experiencing how it was for my grandmother before electric lights were invented. For heat we purchased one of those tube-shaped kerosene stoves, which emitted thick black smoke if not constantly watched and regulated. Winter was coming on.

—3—

A Taste of Shanghai Social Life

During Candida's visit home, her sister invited us to tea. At a distance of nearly fifty years, I can't describe the home's exterior. I remember entering a large, long room, bare of ornamentation. Two large black teakwood chairs, exquisitely carved, sat throne-like against bare walls. As in a dream we moved from this room into the sunny warmth and color of the family's real living quarters. I realized the house held not one family but several.

A winding stairway led past the open doors of apartments on different levels. The families of Candida's two brothers occupied these rooms, independent of each other, yet in solidarity. I remember finally a pleasant, artistically arranged central room, which belonged either to elder brother John, or her sister, Lily. Here sat Candida's grandmother facing her children, grandchildren and guests—queen of the group that afternoon. My eyes wandered in fascination to her feet, which were like a doll's in tiny doll shoes. The excruciating agonies girl children had suffered in this woman's time were inescapable. Candida had told me that her grandmother's feet had been bound with toes turned under at a very young age. I believe the barbarous practice ended in her mother's time.

Grandchildren in all sizes and ages clung shyly to parents. But when asked to sing, all bashfulness vanished and each vied with the others to perform first.

Refreshment time came and we were served tea and cakes by children who were not family members. I asked Candida about them when we were alone.

"They are slaves," she said, embarrassed.

Not willing to believe my ears, I asked if she meant servants. No, she meant slaves. Girl babies were throwaways. Some were left at the doors of orphanages or churches. Some were sold by impoverished families. They generally received good care by families who trained them as maids, cooks and household help.

This may be a good place to mention the importance of the *amah* in the wealthy Chinese child's life. The trusted female servant, or *amah*, was given charge of the child from its infancy. It was she who disciplined, dried the tears, hugged and caressed and comforted. It was she who taught the child table manners and how to dress, and she who presented the child to the parents when they wanted to spend a little time with their child. Like the southern mammy image in our American culture, the *amah* held a high and respected position in the family. Most especially, she held the heart of the family's son or daughter. Grandmothers, too, seemed closer to the children than the parents. Perhaps the aging grandmother, lacking responsibilities in household matters, did the natural thing and edged in on the *amah*'s territory, for grandmothers were much loved.

We were invited by Candida's relatives to a welcome-home dinner. We were amazed to find one corner of the large dining room completely set up for an American dinner from canapés to steak, potatoes and ice cream. Another corner provided a complete Buddhist feast, sans meat, milk and other Buddhist taboos. The majority of guests moved along the center table, which spanned the length of three rooms.

Home at the college again, the three of us chatted awhile about the lovely occasion we had just experienced.

Sister Frederica praised Candida's sister on her graciousness and competence as a hostess. I marveled at the variety and number of delicious fish, meat and vegetable dishes, as well as sauces and pickled vegetables, nuts and cakes I could not name.

"Where in the world does Lily keep all those lovely porcelain serving dishes?" I asked Candida. "She must have hundreds."

Candida explained Lily didn't own all those dishes by any means. Servants in upper-class homes had free rein to engineer such occasions. The servants of friends and neighbors got together when a family hosted a grand affair and loaned out the needed plates and serving dishes. The lady of the house didn't question or worry about getting her own things back. She knew her own servants would see to it the family had "big face," and that is all that mattered. I could see that this state of affairs gave servants the freedom to be creative, to earn the appreciation of their employers and to share the family's face in the eyes of their own peers.

When we arrived in Shanghai, inflation was off to the races. We learned that Chinese National Currency, CNC, was 3,000 to one American dollar the day we arrived. It would escalate rapidly and the exchange would soon be in the millions. It took me a week or two to comprehend what this meant. I learned something about it when a beggar, to whom I handed what I thought was the equivalent of a dollar, threw it on the ground and stepped on it angrily. I found I had given him less than a nickel.

Sister Frederica gave in to our pleas and stayed until after Christmas. The cold had sharpened, and she took us shopping for fur-lined boots that would do much to see us through the Shanghai winter. We were cautioned by the Sacred Heart nuns not to add sweaters or underthings too soon or too many at a time, for we wouldn't have anything to add as the cold increased. But Sister Frederica wisely solicited Candida's sister's know-how and help. Soon we each had what the Chinese wore—padded underwear. The Sacred Heart nuns were similarly prepared. One day we would go down to the chapel to find all the heretofore slim nuns expanded to three times their size. We would know then it was time to pull out all the stops and use all the coverage we had.

After a glorious Christmas Mass in the college chapel and a festive breakfast, we opened a big "Care" package from the sisters in L.A. We each received personal gifts of scarves and gray berets and mittens crocheted or knitted with sisterly thoughtfulness and love. Three Sunkist oranges brought our California home right into the room.

The Russian community celebrated Christmas a week later. Shanghai had both a Russian Orthodox and a Russian Catholic (in union with Rome) church, so the three of us experienced our first Eastern rite Midnight Mass. After the service, we spoke to the pastor, Jesuit Father Wilcox. British, he had volunteered to be ordained for the Russian rite and now served the White Russian Catholic population in China.

He introduced us to three young women from Harbin who were teaching in an elementary school for foreign children. We learned from them that as long as they could, they would hold out from turning Soviet. Not easy, for they were stateless and therefore ineligible for relief dispensed through the Soviet consulate.

About this time we were contacted by an American Vincentian priest, Father Frederick A. McGuire, head of the CWCC, Catholic Welfare Committee of China. This was the Catholic distributing agency for relief supplies from overseas. His co-administrator was a Canadian, Father J.H. McGoey of the Scarborough Foreign Mission Society. By the time the interview was over, Sister Frederica had assigned me to work for this agency. My work would be to investigate and report the needs of about two hundred orphanages to be found in the length and breadth of China.

News of a Chinese sister, trained in the same work, brought the pastor of Shanghai's large St. Peter's Church to ask for Sister Candida's services. His request was granted. Candida and I both had our work cut out for us, to begin after Christmas holidays.

At last the day of Sister Frederica's departure came. Candida and I would be on our own. We knew that two Hungarian sisters and an American would join us in due course. Meanwhile, it was up to us to get started in our assigned work, as well as find and figure ways to finance a convent of our own.

—4—

We Are on Our Own and Work Begins

While Sister Frederica was with us, Sister Candida seemed to be her usual animated cheerful self. However, when only the two of us remained, her subdued manner and long silences plainly showed something was wrong. Soon I learned that her return to China had presented a problem she could never have foreseen ten years earlier. The foreign gray uniform, insignia of her religious commitment, brought insults, spoken for her hearing behind her back or even boldly to her face. Strangers censured her for identifying with Americans by her dress. She would answer back spiritedly that she was a Chinese through and through and her garb was that of a religious, not political, person.

I learned of the anti-American feeling when Chiang Kai-shek's birthday celebration was due. "Don't go out that day," friends warned me. "An American woman was pelted with vegetables by coolies not long ago during a civic holiday." Two or three times a week I would hear the staccato of exploding firecrackers beyond the college gateway and the excited shouts of a crowd. The rhythmic boom of at least one bass drum on the march told me there was indeed a parade. Another civic holiday, I thought, surprised at the frequency of these celebrations. I took the advice of my friends and never went into the street at these times. Only much later did I learn the truth. On parade were criminals being escorted with jeering fanfare to their deaths. They were handcuffed and led to the Bund, each carrying a huge placard that towered above his head, declaring his crime. Usually the crime was theft or dealing in the black market. Age made no difference. Youths of fifteen could be condemned. They were marched to a field beyond the Bund, where each dug his own grave before being shot. Some were probably Communists, or suspected of being so.

The people blamed the American Marines for the steep inflation, I was told. They had overpaid pedicab and ricksha coolies, spending money carelessly and lavishly. This had driven prices up. Now the Marines were gone, but costs still escalated. As time went on and I didn't meet any Americans other than missionaries passing through, I began to recognize that my unique position as a lone American allowed me to disappear in a crowd. Europeans of varied nationalities spoke plainly their own anti-American sentiments as if I were one of them or not there at all. It puzzled me to hear folks from nations we were helping with air-lifted food and medicines speak in disparaging tones or words.

Thus it was that my Alice in Wonderland ignorance of world politics was gradually dissipated. I would never have learned from the Chinese, not even from Candida's cordial and sincerely well-wishing relatives, that anything was amiss in this country I would gladly have made my own. I did hear the word "squeeze" from everyone, but that went with the anger over inflation. We were not blamed for squeeze—the constant forcing up of costs for services as well as goods. I picked up by radar, in a sense, that the government itself was being blamed. And from this, that Chiang was not totally trusted. Handsome, respected by the Western world, the Chinese were proud to have him represent them. He gave face. But without newspapers or commentators, dependent solely on what I picked out of the air, I began to understand that the Chinese people were between the devil and the deep blue sea. If the devil was communism, the deep blue sea was a government that took from them, promised nothing and gave nothing.

As soon as our Superior left, I began preparing a syllabus for a social work class that I would teach to senior sociology majors in return for board and room. Many planned to do graduate work in England or America, and the class would serve as an introduction to the profession of social work, which any one of them might wish to pursue.

I prepared my course outline with utmost confidence, blissfully forgetful that my Chinese students were of an altogether different culture and background. By what they could not understand of Western ways, these wealthy daughters of an upper class were to teach me how far I had to reach to understand China and the people I had been sent to serve! When, for example, I would tell my pretty, fashionably coifed and dressed students that the aim of social work was to help people help themselves, their politely smiling faces were masked questions. What people? Help themselves do what? The only poor they saw were at the lowest extreme, beggars who were helping themselves very well, even as professionals. Household servants? They were well taken care of.

But all this would come up in living color. On paper it looked right and good. I gave the dean my syllabus. She might have warned me, but she only smiled and thanked me. This I was to notice more and more, that experienced missionaries withheld comment and advice. Greenhorn that I was, I would learn the way they had learned, by my own foolish mistakes.

As Candida let drop bits and pieces of news about her work, I knew she was happy in it and felt she was bringing about her dream of introducing the SSS methods. She spoke of a Boys' Club and said they were planning a party. The Mothers' Club, a sewing circle, would provide edibles. When I asked if this meant cake and ice cream, she winced.

"Oh, no," she said. "Sweet things would be a real penance. Nuts and salty crackers they like much better." Again, I learned something about China.

The pastor gave her free rein and expressed special interest in a group of Cantonese teenagers he hoped she would attract and possibly form into a choir. Cantonese and Shanghai people were not usually compatible. It was her task to make the outsiders feel a part of the group. Busy as she was, she was still able to moonlight with a growing adult English class. Her deepest interest, I knew, lay in attracting young women to our society. And sure enough, she began to form a small group of possible vocations.

At nine o'clock on the appointed morning, I reported for work at the Catholic Welfare Committee of China. Its warehouse and offices were within walking distance of the college. I therefore crossed a pretty midtown park, neatly patterned with garden beds. Trees I couldn't identify in their wintry leafless state promised pleasant shade and shadows come spring. This was January and bitingly cold. I saw Chinese men here and there practicing the slow controlled arm and leg movements of traditional Chinese exercises, Tai Chi. A few merely strolled, singly or in pairs. I saw no women and no joggers. Without self-consciousness, a single stroller broke into quiet song even as I passed by.

Within minutes I emerged from the park and the compact, modern square CWCC building stood before me. The doors were opened wide to admit the rapid coming and going of several young Ukrainian men who were unloading a big truck. I found my way to another entrance that revealed a corridor. Midway, I saw a large office that proved to be the one I wanted.

On entering, I found my two employers seated at desks in front of a gigantic map of China. They rose to shake hands, welcoming me cordially and with humor. Father McGuire's graying hair showed he was the older of the two, perhaps in his early forties. He was an American from Boston, and the clerical suit he wore told me he was the one most engaged in public relations. The younger priest, Canadian Father John H. McGoey, of the Scarborough Foreign Mission Society, wore khaki fatigues indicating that he worked directly with the men.

They explained CWCC's function as liaison between the bishops, Catholic hospitals, clinics, and orphanages and international relief supplies. I marveled at the smooth-running operation they outlined. Their achievement in barely a year's time without funds, equipment or coolies had not been easy. But their eyes were so alive with excitement of the challenge, I knew they were loving every minute of its demands on them.

My work, they told me, was to investigate the needs of the orphanages and report back. This meant travel by any means possible—steamer, river boat, train, bus or jeep. From that day and hour began my chance to see the real China.

I was pleasantly surprised to find the orphanages I visited were not the coldly institutionalized buildings I imagined them to be. In the coastal cities of Shanghai, Ningpo and Hangchow at least, they were wooden structures of only one or two stories. Untreated and unpainted, the wood looked gray and weathered. Spacious rooms allowed an informal, family-style mode of living. The children slept in dormitories, according to age groups, with one or more of the older orphans to monitor and keep discipline. A sister slept near in case of illness or other emergency.

"Old orphan" was the term used for those who were not married to farmers or adopted by well-to-do families as servant girls. From birth to death the orphans were sheltered and cared for by the nuns. They earned their keep as auxiliary helpers for the nuns if no golden opportunity opened a door for them to the outside world. A distinct area of the orphanage was called the crêche and used for infants dropped off or brought to the orphanage door.

Here, the old orphans greatly helped the sister in charge with laundering, feeding, bathing and changing the infants' diapers.

The nuns told me they had continued to carry on their work during the Japanese occupation. The Daughters of Charity of St. Vincent de Paul were well known in Japan and respected highly. They continued on with the orphanages, largely dependent on their own small farming and the generosity of villagers, who shared their scant food. They also continued with their clinical services despite the lack of medical supplies and equipment.

Prior to my first visit to an orphanage, whether it was in Shanghai or another city, I wanted very much to take toys or games to the children. The missionary priest advised me to be careful. The Chinese children could turn almost any game into gambling. This ruled out marbles and even checkers, if I could have found checkers in the stores. I finally resorted to a basketball and balls for playing catch. Jump rope was another possibility, I thought, and took along three or four. Of course, these were not enough, and I was to find that among the hundreds of children of varying ages, really the best I could do was teach Western games like hide-and-seek or, for the older children, parlor games. With the help of my students I did this to some extent before I realized that the children had more fun entertaining me with their own songs and games than in learning mine. And I certainly had more fun as the entertainee than as a misplaced group worker. As I had noticed earlier in the Wei family home, Chinese children have great spontaneity, sense of humor and eagerness to perform in song and dance.

I think the best way to describe my experience in the orphanages is to share with the readers my own letters written during my visits to the Ningpo and Chosan orphanages. Two of these letters, preserved over nearly fifty years, follow.

—5—

Letters Home, 1947

Shipboard, May 15, 1947

Dearest Sisters Back Home:

   Here I am aboard this trim French steamer bound for Ningpo, an overnight trip. We are just leaving Shanghai—about 200 Chinese passengers and one lone foreigner—me. This is a modern ship and I am well established in a cabin all to myself, with the landscape slipping rapidly past my window. The solicitous Chinese cabin boy is an ex-merchant marine who wandered as far as England and married a British girl, so he speaks fluent English.

   Our doors are locked until tickets are collected, and I am impatiently waiting to go on deck in the soft evening light. As I told you in my last letter, I am to spend one week in Ningpo and a day or two at Chosan Island. I will spend a few days in each of three orphanages, two for girls and one for boys. Each orphanage, I should explain, has a complete section for infants. This is called the crêche, undoubtedly named by French nuns since earliest work in China. My job with CWCC is to check out their needs (canned milk and diapers for infants, all manner of canned food and clothing for others) and then supply them from IRA, International Relief goods. The Chosan visit will give me another boat trip, five hours long—this time in a small native boat.

Interruption.... My room was just invaded by a delegation of two Chinese officers demanding my ticket. I produced, delegation left. Door closed. Loud pounding, new and larger delegation at door demanding my passport. I produced. Great business of inspecting same and spelling my name slowly, distinctly and incorrectly. They have gone now so I'm off for a brisk walk on deck.

Later.... Returned to cabin and found cabin boy had been here ahead of me. Light was turned on, shutters were drawn, and a teapot of hot water had been set in the wash bowl. If he meant for me to drink it, I had other ideas—I washed in it. Two cups don't wash much off. Lights out now. To sleep, perhaps to dream, but certainly to rise at four A.M. in order to disembark at five.

•

Crèche de l'Enfant Jesus, Ningpo, May 17, 1947

Yesterday was a beautiful morning! Out on deck in the dawn. The narrow Ningpo River rippled like yellow silk in our ship's wake. Quiet green fields stretched on either side of the river with silver fog softening every outline.

Two Sisters of Charity met the boat in rickshas to bring me here. This is a girls' orphanage, badly damaged by Japanese bombing but still in condition to house 296 children and personnel. Babies left at the door are often still unwashed from childbirth, and one that arrived while I was present had a note pinned on it saying it had not eaten in days. It began to die and was at once baptized the name I gave it, Marie.

The girls range in years from birth to marriageable age. If people only knew how all hands have to work just to survive! The children even make string. From brushwood in the fields and bamboo they make the kitchen utensils and scrubbing brushes. Some garments are so patched the original piece of goods is the same size as the patch.

Not a soul speaks English here. My French is improving vastly, together with Italian, Spanish and Chinese. Every sentence I speak includes five languages plus my hands, face, arms and shoulders. Last night, by the way, I slept in a French bed so swathed in mosquito netting I had to ask how to get into it.

Arose at 5:30 A.M., prayed in the large French chapel until six, when a priest from the Cathedral said Mass. The orphans attended, singing the rosary and what must have been several litanies at the top of their lungs.

At nine, the Sister Superior of the boys' orphanage came to fetch me in a ricksha. More than 400 live in this enormous place. The buildings here, like those of the girls' orphanage, are concrete or cement, and very long corridors join one section to another. It is so big I could never find my way around it alone. Before the war (WWII) it housed a thousand.

The sisters never turn away a soul—old, blind, young, all may come. One time three old men wanted to enter, but the sisters explained they had nothing to give them to eat. They slept on the doorstep night after night until the police asked the sisters to take them. When the Superior told them they were short on food, the police said, "Never mind, we'll get you some." As soon as the sisters agreed to take the men, three piculs (over 400 pounds!) of rice arrived on their doorstep. Only divine aid could be keeping these sisters going. They are surely doing everything they can just to keep their people sheltered and fed. They are so thankful for the IRA aid—which comes in the nick of time for all of these child-care "homes."

Tomorrow I embark at six for Chosan Island. Pirates

have held up two boats lately. I'm told my boat will be small and thoroughly native, with no modern conveniences whatsoever. The trip is only five hours under good conditions. It is raining right now, so I wonder what will conditions be!

•

Tinghai, Chosan Island, May 18, 1947

Now you know where I am. Perhaps I am in heaven. How beautiful it is! Early this morning the Superior accompanied me to the boat—so small and so crammed with humanity! A missionary priest accompanied me to Chosan. We sat in a cabin filled with Chinese men, two women, and one little boy whom I held on my lap most of the way. He was so sleepy and had no place else to sit. His mother stood most of the time. I gave her my place while I stood on the deck awhile, but the rain drove me back, as well as the lack of room (even on deck). It was not a deck at all—just a narrow passageway, traversed every five minutes by enterprising passengers with edible wares to sell on board.

One of the most interesting aspects of the whole trip was the entertainment. Wandering minstrels, just like the Middle Ages! Yes, they tell me that the storyteller is an institution inseparable from Chinese life. The boat had not started before a thin, brown-skinned Chinese stood up in the small room and began a kind of chant, accompanying himself on a Chinese violin. At first not a soul paid attention to him, but he went on and on. Then, when he had the room's attention he threw himself into his story, punctuating his chapters with a little cat-like tune and wild ditty on the violin. This lasted 20 minutes perhaps. Another man followed with a recitation that lasted quite a long while and the boat was well on its way by the finish.

The next storyteller was a desiccated, wrinkled old man accompanied by a tiny girl whose face was powdered and rouged. She wore bracelets, earrings and other ornaments and a jacket of shiny red satin. I assumed she was the old man's granddaughter. When he came to a pause in the story and played an "intermission number" on three clacking sticks, she passed a little box around the crowd for donations. During his story she stood close to me. I reassured her with smiles and tried to talk with her in Shanghai dialect, which she did not speak. Ningpo speech is far different from Shanghai. To my dismay I learned from the missionary that she was not the man's granddaughter, but a slave. These little slaves are children not wanted by their parents—perhaps sold, perhaps left to die as infants. Their fate is not always bad, for they are often cared for in good families in return for service. However, in the case of a girl, the fate is not hard to imagine.

By this time the big round table in the middle of the room had been filled with glasses of hot tea, cakes and watermelon seeds. The people ate all the way, all the time. About ten o'clock, fish and meat were sold by vendors who trod on our toes without apology. About 11:30, bowls of rice and soup were passed over our trembling heads. Every hour or so two men came in with hot, wet towels and everyone washed hands and face.

The small boy on my lap wore a metal ring around his neck to keep away evil spirits. It also meant long life. We were a happy family for five hours on that boat. Gorgeous scenery passed by, but the sky was dark and rain intermittent. We did not see much.

•

Chosan Island, May 18, 1947

I had a royal reception at the orphanage here. The Superior is Belgian, but speaks English. There is only one other foreign sister, the other 11 are Chinese. The compound is composed of several buildings made of mortar or concrete. Japanese occupation ruined them and they have been repaired only badly. The whole place is enclosed by its own wall, plus on one side, the city wall. These walled cities are wonderful to see. The wall around Tinghai was built to keep out bandits, and it is much lower than it used to be because of the damage from bombs. I spent almost an hour in the garden, which is lovely, and was amused to see from the corner of my eye a cluster of small heads with eyes watching me. I am a walking, talking zoo to the children here. There are four foreigners on the island now that I am here—a priest, two sisters and myself. Everywhere I go I am followed by a bevy of little girls, chattering and giggling about me.

Later... It is now afternoon. All morning I spent surveying the orphanage. They call it that, but the children have parents somewhere probably. One girl was left to die because her hair grows straight up. That is a sign of the Fox Spirit. Most were abandoned as infants because of their sex alone. Boys are left to die if they have physical defects of any kind. Besides 200 dependent children there are many adults here, as in Ningpo. Blind—about 30 girls. Elderly—about 15 women and 40 men. (Idiots, crippled, mutes—all are kept in an orphanage.) A dispensary almost bare of medicines takes care of charity cases from the town and countryside.

The sisters lack everything to do with. This is poorer than the Ningpo orphanages because it is so cut off from every source of aid. There is absolutely no way to wash the children without great inconvenience. The water must be brought from the river, which is quite far, and there are no tubs nor specially made rooms for bathing.

Now I must go with *Ma Soeur* and the parish priest to a house out in the country. We are walking, so I am borrowing a pair of shoes made by the children. They make everything they wear or use. From my window here I look over the curved roofs to the curved slopes of the green hills. Below in the patio an old man dozes and a dozen rabbits are blinking in the sun.

•

Later... I am speechless! If only you could see what I have seen! Why have we never heard how beautiful China is? The beauty is unimaginable. The coloring is beyond belief.

We walked right through the city gate, and were accosted by an old woman or two, demanding where we were going and how old we were, just out of sheer friendliness. The narrow stone passageway that leads to the countryside took us between one-storied, almost windowless stone houses, joined together. Once past these homes the glorious countryside opened up. Stone graves, built up like small houses on top of the ground, were everywhere. They were spaced some distance from each other and set at random on the green hills and flat plain.

The farms are also granite buildings, encircled by a brick wall. We walked along stone pathways between the watery rice fields. Every inch of the fields is being used here, so it is all neat and orderly to the eye. Buttercups and forget-me-nots and some purplish flower like clover blossoms dance along the pathways between these cultivated rice fields. Black water buffalo pull the farmer's plow through the wet field, and the farmer himself wades along behind the beast. We had to step aside now and then to let a man carrying a bamboo pole with a basket of grain on either end pass by. One man was thus carrying two dead pigs.

We stopped to rest in an old mission church where Mass is said every Sunday. Once it was very nice—but now? Japanese used it for a fortress. They tried to break the cross on the rooftop. Four men worked on it to break it, but could do no more than twist it back—as it is now.

We stopped again to visit a Christian farmer's family. The children were all healthy and bright-eyed. The wife gave us tea and dried sweet potatoes. Sweet potatoes grow plentifully and when they are sliced thin and salted they are candy for the people here. Outdoors on the ground lay the fish being dried in the sun. Several girls were drying beans, peas and meat.

    At last we came to the house—once a lovely place, high on a hill where the view was superb. We sat on the porch, carefully avoiding boards that threatened to catapult us down the hill faster than we came up. Below us, we saw the farmers working, the goats browsing, the cows meditating, all near a cluster of houses.

    To my delight, we saw a funeral procession about to begin. The beating of a tin pan announced the sad occasion. We knew a very poor person had died because there was only one chief mourner, a little girl in white. Two children preceded the coffin, banging the tin pan for a gong. Two men carried the wooden, unpainted coffin, slung on bamboo poles over their shoulders. As soon as the procession left the path from the houses, a third man lighted a fire on the path so that the soul of the departed could not return to haunt.

    The procession began to climb right up the hill toward us. A man who seemed to be a hired grave finder ran on ahead up the hill to find a spot to leave the coffin. And when the two pall bearers saw him ascend the hill—they struck! Yes. Down they sat in the middle of the path and refused to budge. Loud voices, a few jokes, bargaining. They would not move without more pay. The chief mourner stood beside the coffin, now abandoned on the path, while the gong beaters followed the grave finder around. Then another man appeared with a food offering for the dead. The chief mourner got tired of waiting around and began to play with two small boys who happened by. An hour later, the situation hadn't changed. We knew that before nightfall they probably set the coffin on the hill and piled rocks over it, put food in front of it, and scolded the little mourner into a fit of sorrow. *Requiescat in pace.*

Going home we walked back by another path to a little red barge waiting for us on the river. However, the boatman had been lured to a friend's house for a nip of wine. We found him there, and he arose with alacrity to come and propel our small barque around the city wall. What peace! The silence has to be listened to like a song. In the twilight of the day, winding in and out among the fields with the hills undulating around us, it was like resting in the center of an enormous flower with the hills for petals. As we approached the city wall, we passed stone huts built right on the river bank. We could see the happy families inside, with chickens and other pets stepping familiarly in and out of the doorways along with the children. The wall hides the city completely except for here and there a curved rooftop. Communists hide in these hills, and I understand that 120 of them have come into the city now. Someday trouble will come here.

Later... Now to catch up, with four days unrecorded (in this world, that is). I am sailing homeward as I write, sitting on the edge of my bed in my little cabin while the evening sun beats into my room. Yes, it is nearly seven and yet the sun is hot and high. I stayed in Chosan until Thursday. Tuesday was a quiet day and I tried to write my reports. Wednesday I was free and yet could not return to Ningpo, for *Ma Soeur* wanted to go with me next day. So early, after 5:30 Mass, I went with a Chinese sister and a swarthy boatman up the silent river in a little barque. We silently and slowly cut through the canal waters to another island. We got out and walked through fairyland until we sighted the other side, where another little boat waited for us across a rushing stream to carry us to a smaller island. Boats being useless without boatmen, and our own boatman lacking the magnetic power to bring the boat to us by sheer hypnotic will-power, we resorted to shouting. This worked. Leaping over the mountains came two long legs with a boy attached. He crossed to us in a trice, and soon we were over on his island—a small hill covered with flowers, wheat, ferns, trees, and topped by a little gray house. We spent two hours here, reading and walking. The view of the surrounding islands is indescribable. You have to come and see.

   Next day we rose at four and departed for Ningpo. Our boat was small, crowded, and much like the one that brought me from Ningpo to Chosan. This time I held a sleeping girl on my motherly lap. People were nervous on this trip, for pirates recently held up the same boat.
   We landed at noon, and I went by ricksha to the girls' orphanage. In late afternoon the orphans, the blind, and old people came for service in the chapel. How they pray! Yards and yards of prayers they sing by the hour. The children adore to pray. At Chosan I noticed how they sing their prayers from twilight to pitch dark without a pause, just because they like to. All by themselves they will begin to sing loudly a couple of rosaries for this and a couple of litanies for that.
   In the huge parish church I saw things I never saw before in church. The big pillars lining the aisles were brilliantly painted like candy canes. On closer inspection I saw that the striped rings were really colorful grapes encircling the big columns. Spittoons are furnished for the congregation but seldom used. The floor is handier and not so easy to miss.
   I will never forget how wonderful these sisters have been to me. Nothing was left undone in thoughtfulness, and they are so genuinely cordial and friendly.

•

Now I am on my way home. Last night I said goodnight to some of my Ningpo children. Played ball with the little ones and found them a lively bunch. The Chosan children are even livelier. I think I enjoyed them the most. The night I visited the two- and three-year-olds, I was amazed at their precocity. They had not gone to bed, being occupied with praying in their dormitory, besides tending to the needs of nature—not much of a problem to people in China, anywhere, anytime! Anyway, these tots bowed to me like tiny mandarins and then swept me out of the room onto the veranda to see the moon rise. They brought me a tiny chair that put me on the exact level with their heads and then they danced about me like Lilliputians with a captured Gulliver. If you could only see how small they are! Chubby and short—so cute.

You may wonder what happens after the orphans are grown up. This is the way a girl is married. The parents of a young Christian farmer come to the orphanage and ask for a wife. The girls of proper age then file past a window and the parents choose one. The worst of it is, that poor as the orphanages are, they are palatial compared to the farmer's home to which the bride goes. One girl came crying back to the sisters because her husband's house had dirt floors (the usual thing). She was accustomed to cement or wood. As for the boys' orphanage, the orphans are taught carpentry or whatever the institution does for its livelihood.

Wish you were all here to see China. I love it.

Lovingly in Christ,
Sister Mariel

—6—

Fieldwork for My Students

At no time in my coastal journeys nor at home again in Shanghai did I hear more than faint rumors of war. Only by the hindsight of a history learned much later would I know that in March 1947 Chiang's army was jubilant over the capture of Mao's headquarters at Yenan. Mao had then moved his troops into the backcountry of Shansi Province and began to plan his counteroffensive. His main objective was to eliminate the strength of the Nationalist forces rather than to acquire land or villages. He also planned to cut off the north-south railway lines that moved through north China.

Back on the homefront I met with my senior sociology majors twice a week at the last class period of the day. Living in the college as we did, I had only to walk down a hall and climb a stair and I was there.

Since postwar heating had not been installed, my students sat through class in Western-style fur coats over colorful Chinese dresses. I was surprised to see how strongly some of them resembled the pretty Mexican teenagers of my Youth Club in L.A. I wondered how serious they were about social work and suspected they took my class mainly for the novelty of watching an American perform.

My immediate concern was that they understand my English. I was careful to ask the class after each explanation or instruction I gave if the meaning was clear to all. Invariably the students nodded and smiled that yes, they did understand. To make sure that they did, I gave a test on the first week's subject matter and learned to my dismay that they certainly had not understood a great deal. But why, then, did they all say they did understand? I finally learned the answer.

"But we did not want to make you lose face, Sister," a student told me when pressed for the truth. "If we say we do not understand, we say you do not make clear to us." Oh, dear. After that, I always asked a student to translate into Chinese instructions I wanted to emphasize.

It didn't take more than two or three sessions to discover that I desperately needed help to make case work meaningful to these intelligent young women. From their polite, blank expressions and utter silence when I asked if they had questions, I realized I was offering them a course in Western, not Asian, problems.

When I asked them to give me an example of a family problem one girl suggested jealousies between the number-two wife and the acknowledged proper wife. That did it for me. I had to put these girls in touch with a greater variety of emotional problems within their own culture.

Field work in an agency had been an integral part of my own training. Shanghai had no casework agency. So I told the girls we must create one. They would meet the poor as individuals. They would sit down with a peasant mother and tactfully find out her problems over and beyond those of food and clothing. They would keep a record of each interview and follow it up with a home visit to the family. The girls were enthusiastic.

At the warehouse we had extra offices, and I was given the use of one of these, along with permission to store supplies in the same facility. This would be a tiny step in the direction of getting some of those UNRRA (United Nations Relief and Rehabilitation Agency) relief goods to the people. Although my two bosses teased me about diving head-first where angels fear to tread, I knew they hoped for the best and wished me well.

I had an office which we would call Catholic Social Services. Now I needed commodities for our clients. Through Candida's brother I obtained an interview with Shanghai's Mayor Wu. I can't remember his office. Instead I recall vividly talking with him in the back seat of his chauffeured limousine on the way to the Shanghai docks. He was a serious man who seemed to have a heavy burden, saddening his expression. This sadness I would see increasingly in the faces of businessmen. He was pleased that I was trying to involve educated young women in problems peculiar to their own land. He asked me pointedly if we would be able to get the UNRRA food and clothing to the people. I assured him we would. After showing me around the crates and bales lying on the dock, he told me he would arrange for an army truck to take me to the supplies on call.

As we picked our way among the clothing and crates of foodstuffs, I sensed more than sadness in the mayor's expression. Perhaps I imagined a certain grim hardening of the lines around his mouth. I had seen this same look of concerned gravity in the eyes of other businessmen. On the bus, on the street, in the bank where I waited at a window for service of the teller, the silent, closed faces and compressed lips of middle-aged successfully employed men spoke to me of...what? I began to judge that it spoke of disillusionment in their own government and fear for the future of family and country.

I remembered comments that UNRRA goods went to thieves and pilferers. Chiang had insisted on handling the distribution of UNRRA goods, but had done little more than warehouse them. Through the concerted efforts of Protestant and Catholic missionaries he was now allowing the churches and consulates to access supplies for their own missions and institutions. The needy Chinese themselves were forgotten. That, I knew, must be a painful realization for patriots who sincerely wanted Chiang to be their leader.

We had an office and relief commodities. Now, we

needed a secretary and a way to pay her. Because of my travels to orphanages I needed someone full-time in charge of the office and supplies. She must be paid, I felt, not a volunteer, so I could depend on her.

The answer to my first need, a secretary, was Rowena. Already a graduate of Aurora College, a sociology major, she was saving money to go to an American university. Tall, with black hair, shoulder length and softly waved, she looked the ideal of China's new young woman. I enjoyed her ready laugh and witty humor, but most of all her Southern accent. I wondered who taught her English, for she might have come from Alabama, if not Texas. She called me "Sistah...." She was delighted to have the job and, after attending my class on record-keeping, took over the complete functioning of the office as long as we were able to keep it operating.

If I could pay her in U.S. currency, fifty dollars a month would be plenty, Rowena said. With inflation escalating like mad, I knew she would have a tremendous return on the black market. But how to get the fifty dollars? Candida came to my rescue. Again, her brother waved his magic wand, and Candida and I met with a group of the city's foremost businessmen and merchants to form a board for the new agency. Like Mayor Wu, they were very pleased that Chinese students would be urged and inspired to work for China. So many went to foreign universities but did not use their education and expertise for their own country. Candida explained to them the work of our community and I knew she, too, was hoping for their future support.

With everything finally in place, I told my students that now we must clean the office, maybe paint it, and get ready for work. Each member of the class must spend time at the office, interviewing one or two clients in as much depth as appropriate, given the limited time. They must bundle packages of food and clothing, and record both the interview and the items given out. Understood? Yes, Sister.

On Saturday at the specified hour, probably ten, I was at the office. Rowena came in with her big smile and immense goodwill. No one else came. Thus I learned that I had asked daughters of the wealthiest families of Shanghai to come down and clean, wash windows and maybe paint the office. Was I out of my mind? But they said "yes." Of course they did. Did they want me to lose face by saying no? So Rowena and I cleaned. We did not paint. We packaged food and clothing. And to my dismay, dragged from the bales party dresses, evening gowns, beaded blouses, high-heeled shoes. We opened crates of chocolate syrup (Chinese don't like it). At some of the foodstuffs, Rowena and I looked at each other and burst out laughing. Sauerkraut? Well, maybe...but gallon jars of strawberry jam? I remembered how Candida's boys' club preferred nuts and salty things to sweets. Evidently, our generous countrymen had donated as blindly to the poor of China as I had begun teaching social problems the Chinese had already solved in their own way.

That afternoon we hung out a sign. Rowena had a good desk provided by the CWCC fathers. We were in business. That evening I told Candida about the impossible clothing. "Give them to my Mothers' Club and they will use them to make padded garments."

Wonderful! That is exactly what we did and, since it was deep winter, the mothers knew they were doing a much-needed charity.

I struggled on to enlighten my students about problems, emotional or domestic, as unreal to them as moon rocks. Hunger was what they saw in the faces that met them at the office, personal hunger and concern for the hunger of children and relatives. At least the girls may have learned compassion. Maybe this was the best beginning they could have had for a useful concern for others. I hoped it was so.

—7—

The Russian Connection

Almost as soon as our Social Service Office opened its doors, the pastor of the Russian Catholic Church paid us a visit. Father Wilcox was a short, stocky man with compassionate brown eyes and a beard. His worried frown told us this was no social call. His congregation was largely White Russians and therefore stateless. The Soviet consulate only took care of Russians with Soviet passports. Although pastors had access to supplies, Father Wilcox had no truck to pick them up, no space for storage and no personnel for organized distribution.

At the time of the Russian Revolution in 1917, those who sided with the Tsar took the white background of the royal flag for their emblematic color. The Bolsheviks had chosen red. For this reason the term "White Russian" designated the fleeing nobility, gentry and intelligentsia, as well as members of the Russian Orthodox Church. At this time only China opened her doors to these penniless refugees. Thousands fled by foot or by Trans-Siberian Railroad to Manchuria on the northern border of China and Russia, forming a stable settlement at Harbin.

Although now, in 1947, Mao's Communist forces were still held at bay headquartered at Yenan, the Russian settlers correctly believed that his intended goal was Manchuria. The exodus from Harbin had begun shortly before our arrival in October 1946. In March of 1947 Yenan fell to the Nationalists. But from every indication, the Communists were using the defeat to cover their continuing push northward, ever northward.

Father Wilcox was now asking us to help his parishioners. To me, their need instantly gave a use for the Western clothing so unsuitable for the Chinese. Shoes, with their hard leather soles and string laces, could not be considered for Chinese men, women or children, who wore flat cloth slippers universally. The foodstuffs so incompatible with Asian stomachs were entirely suited to Russian tastes. Although we were both dismayed and amused at the inappropriateness of the food selections, we knew that the contributing countries had intended to please, as much as to feed, the victims of a long war. If the Chinese had been donors to a Western country, no doubt they would have sent what they themselves most enjoyed on the table. And so had we. But much money could have been spent more wisely on rice, soups and vegetables when we were planning our Care gifts for China. As it was, our foods were eaten. The black market sold back to Shanghai's foreign population what the Chinese would not have cared for anyway. Not all was stolen, of course. The missionaries and consulates were diligently serving people in their care.

All we needed to open another agency would be office space and a staff. A brief consultation with my employers gained us the office we needed, and I asked Father Wilcox to find me three or four young women for staff. I told him we could pick up the relief goods for his church when the army truck picked up our own and, in fact, we could probably share with him much of what the crates and bales contained. He left us with his eyes shining. He promised me the young ladies would soon be in touch with me.

The next day they came—Ludmila, Kristina, Catherine and Anya. We held our first meeting in our own office. I had met Kristina and her sister Catherine at Christmas, at which time they were teaching. They had been subsequently fired when they refused to take out Soviet passports. Anya was married and had a little girl. Ludmila was single, unemployed and dying to be office manager. All agreed that she should be. She was a very outgoing, bubbly young woman, probably near thirty-five but with a youthful, ingenue appearance. Warm and friendly, she seemed the natural leader of the group.

During those first days in Shanghai, when Sister Frederica and I had explored the city's streets and lanes, I learned with a shock the power of the stereotype. Russians were here. Russians were passing me on the sidewalks, browsing beside me in department stores. I had never seen a Russian in real life. The earliest pictures I had seen were newspaper cartoons in 1917. I was six then and couldn't miss the cartoons while I scrambled through news pages looking for the funny paper. The caricatured Russian was always labeled "Bolshevik." He was fat and had a bushy black beard, fat arms and a fat bomb in his fat hand. That is a Russian, clicked the memory in my little brain. And then nothing ever happened to bring me face to face with a living Russian. Movies? Books? If anyone had asked me what I thought of Russians, I would have given a non-prejudiced reply. But all the time, I now knew, the bomb-clutching image would have given my answer the lie. So when I met the young Russian women at the church, I was ashamed to find myself astonished at their richly warm humanity.

Here with my volunteer staff, I felt very much at ease and at home. Catherine, the older of the two sisters, was a large-boned Brunhilde. Kristina was tall and slender, with finely chiseled features. Anya was small, wiry and brown-haired. Her little girl, blond like her Russian father, was between five and six years old, and attended the school under Soviet auspices from which Kristina and Catherine were fired. The sisters lived with their mother, a widow. Their grandfather had been a priest of the Eastern rite Catholic Church, which permits a married priesthood. Ludmila never gave a clear picture of her circumstances, but I assumed she lived with family members.

Before we talked of anything else, we faced the problem of paying Ludmila the salary of a full-time office manager. At once, she had a solution. A musical stage play in Russian. The others agreed, eyes dancing with enthusiasm and anticipation. They already had performed a musical in Harbin. Ludmila had been the star. They all sang and still knew the parts they had played. The girls would notify several young Ukrainian men who had had roles in the previous cast. Catherine and Ludmila would hire the church hall, which had a good stage. They would charge admission and advertise that the play was for funds to aid the White Russians. I should worry about nothing. They would take care of everything.

The excitement infected me as much as it did them. I did not forget to announce that we all must meet on a day agreed upon to clean and perhaps paint the office. This group would not disappoint me. They were long used to rolling up their sleeves and attacking a given space with mops and buckets.

As they promised, I had nothing to do but enjoy the play. Their advertising (mostly word of mouth) brought a packed auditorium on the night of the first performance. Soviets as well as White Russians came. Many held Soviet passports, not from conviction but from need of benefits denied the stateless.

Ludmila sang her role in a clear, lilting soprano. The leading man, a baritone, was handsome. Catherine and Anya had speaking as well as singing parts. Pretty Kristina was not wasted, although her role was in the chorus. Cheers and applause attested to the success of everyone involved. Box office receipts amply covered Ludmila's salary for the first two months.

Since the play had been presented on Saturday night, the next morning the cast and I attended church together, then met in the big hall for a celebration breakfast. The hall had been cleared, swept, and the tables decorated with crêpe paper streamers. We all drank toasts (tea or coffee) to the leading actors and applauded short, pithy speeches. When Catherine announced what the play had netted us, the hall rang with cheers. I remember thanking the actors, ticket sellers, ushers and everyone who had contributed to our success. Then pancakes, if I recall correctly, were put before us; we ate and, at the end, sang. I will never forget the cascade of songs, one after another as if rehearsed to be sung in sequence—although they were wholly spontaneous. They sang in Russian or Ukrainian. The sunshine poured through the windows, the singing turned light into music. In that hour it seemed inconceivable that the entire world was not a haven of peace.

For an hour on a Sunday morning in March 1947, God was in His heaven and all seemed right with the world. But at that very moment or near it, Chiang's army was taking Yenan, enemy Mao's headquarters. The civil war raged on. In Europe, the Hungarian sister who was named to head this China branch, could not get out. Our Superior General was in acute danger of arrest for her denunciation of Communist policies and her influence on her fellow countrymen and women. But it all seemed out of sight, out of mind, far away...especially with no input of news reports. All that alerted me to suspect that all was not right with the world was the sadness I saw in Chinese faces.

That was Sunday. On Monday, Ludmila and her coworkers painted a sign on wood that said: CATHOLIC SOCIAL SERVICES—FOR WHITE RUSSIANS ONLY.

—8—

Jeep Adventures

One of the most glorious surprises was the gift of a brand-new Willys Jeep, sent by the Oakland branch of the St. Vincent de Paul Society. This is a world-wide benevolent society of laymen, whose purpose is to help the poor and sick. From then on I drove to cities like Hangchow that were easily accessible by well-restored roads.

The jeep allowed me to see much more of real China than travel by steamer or bus. Usually one or more of my students accompanied me. Over the years, Candida had given me lessons in Shanghai-ese, but dialects differed radically from one city to another. I visited Hangchow more than once, for it was a sizable city. It may have been there that I experienced a leprosarium as well as a clinic, hospital and orphanage under Catholic auspices.

The leprosarium impressed me unforgettably, mainly because of the nature of the illness. In biblical times, the leper was cast out of society without pity or help. Down the ages this has ceased to be true, but mystery clings to the name of the disease. We know it is not easily transmitted, but we still don't quite know how to handle it socially.

A handsome young Chinese, probably in his thirties, was in charge of the recreational program the day I was there. He was not disfigured at all, except for the lion look. Across the nose to the temples there began an almost imperceptible swelling until the somewhat flattened aspect of a lion's face emerged. I understood that this was typical in the early stage of leprosy. I had been told of white patches that signaled leprosy, but these might be covered by clothing. No one paid attention to the presence of an outsider. The men played cards, laughing and joking. Some held cards between stumps of fingers. The women chatted among themselves, seated apart from the men by choice, not segregation. I don't recall if any knitted or sewed. Facial disfigurations were common, and I didn't like to look into their faces long, lest they be sensitive. I believe the Protestant churches had the majority of leprosaria in China. The orphanages and clinics seemed to be the Catholic province.

I remember Hangchow as the lovely city that reminded me of Pasadena, California, with its clean, wide streets in residential districts and well-kept green lawns. We climbed rows of white stone steps to an enormous temple. Gigantic gods and goddesses gazed serenely down upon us. Some were seated in the lotus position, some stood, all were arrayed in carved garments of somber green or bronze hues. Worshippers looked pygmy-sized as they knelt before or silently walked among these immensities.

In Hangchow we visited several factories. One was a fan factory, another a pharmaceutical enterprise where we saw the horns of a deer, which was used as the basis for a medicine. The sisters' convent was on a hill overlooking the city and a river that Marco Polo is said to have traveled.

I stayed three or four days at the orphanage, which operated a clinic. I asked the sisters if I could be of help in the clinic, under their direction, for I had no nursing skills. Each morning the nuns stood behind long tables sheltered from sun or rain by a canopy. They placed their medicines, bandages, scissors or whatever tools they would need on these tables. Already the people were waiting in long lines, which slowly began to move forward. My job was to hand a sister whatever she asked for. Since none of the sisters spoke English, this drew on my wits with a vengeance.

Finally, she gave me sole charge of one middle-aged man with an elephantine leg. Below the knee it was a large, gray, shapeless stump. At the base of this stump were some toes, which alone revealed the presence of a foot. The sister told me to get a pail of hot water, which I managed to understand and to execute. She then told the man to put his leg in the pail. Then, into the water she squeezed about an inch of clear gel. He sat with leg immersed until the water cooled and the sister told him he could go now. She God-blessed him, smiled, patted his shoulder, and he left us with a serene face and confidence in his step.

Afterward, I looked at the tube and found it was no more than Vaseline. I understood. The medications were gone. In many cases, like this one, all they could give was hope and a blessing. That was what the CWCC was for—to try to get medications (as well as food and clothing) to our impoverished missions and their people.

The orphanage was near the church, and from its pastor, Father Claasen, a Dutch missionary, I learned much about China and its people. He had been a missionary for thirty years and was highly esteemed by the Chinese. He was tall and lean and purposely cultivated a long gray beard which gained him the additional reverence given to old age. He was active in the city's social welfare meetings, which were always ecumenical. I attended one or two of the meetings, where we discussed our agencies' problems of supply and demand. There had always been cooperation among the various denominations here, as in Shanghai.

The misconception in the West that Catholics and Protestants would scrap over the distribution of international relief goods had led the U.N. and Washington to turn a deaf ear to the suggestion that missionaries be in charge of the distribution. Instead they had honored Chiang's request that the Nationalist government handle relief. The government had done nothing. Desperate, the missionaries convinced Chiang that they could do what he had no time for. They could at least take care of the needy in their own missions. What they and the consulates did not distribute had apparently been stockpiled in warehouses scattered about the provinces.

There were no service stations at all in small villages, of course, and even in cities there were few. On another trip to Hangchow, I decided to stay over an extra day and night in order to explore the city further and to visit its beautiful Buddhist temple. I didn't want to burden the nuns with an extra day of serving us meals and therefore found a hotel westernized in plumbing and all other areas for the attraction of foreign tourists. Not willing to trust my can of gasoline to anyone, I asked the hotel manager to have it brought to my room. Instead, he assured me he would lock it in his office for safekeeping. Next morning, one of his employees brought it to my car and lodged it firmly behind the front seat.

About a mile outside of Shanghai, I ran out of gas. Not to worry. My student hopped out on one side of the car and I on the other, confident we were about to fill up the tank. I reached for the container and it almost jumped into my hand, light as a...what? Light as an empty can it was, and it was empty or almost empty. The hotel owner had thoughtfully left a gallon, on which I rolled into Shanghai and, eventually, into our own garage.

The real China I sought and saw in my journeys by jeep could be found in lovely landscapes, green with spring, colorful with blossoming trees. I found it, too, in the stone grave markers scattered on hillsides, as if sown by the wind or birds, never in regimented rows. Little farmhouses here and there came alive with an entire family, from small children to grandmothers, engaged in the industry of survival. Some plowed a field, some dug in vegetable plots, some spread sweet potatoes in the sun to dry. Villages particularly gave me my China. Streets were scarcely wider than my vehicle, and I moved very slowly to avoid chickens, pigs and the people themselves to whom the streets properly belonged and not at all to automobiles. My creeping progress gave children the chance to peer into the jeep's front and rear seats with eyes that shone with excited curiosity. The sound of my horn emboldened one young lad to reach right in front of me and honk it himself. Others wanted to climb on the hood, so I stopped midway in one such village while my student briefly warned the entire street, adults and children together, to stand clear of this dangerous monster called JEEP.

"Jeep! Jeep!" the children chorused, at the same time giving us the thumbs up sign, or crying "Ding Hao." Meaning, of course, we were the tops. By "we," the student said, they meant America.

On these journeys from our Shanghai base to various orphanages in the coastal cities, I pondered the difference between the East and the West, meaning by this the Oriental soul and the Caucasian. I wondered if we would or could ever understand each other. I would be convinced at the end of that first year that we could not.

When I remember my trips between towns by jeep, one hazardous quarter-hour stands out. The roads generally were in very good repair between Shanghai and Hangchow, but after a heavy rain I found short stretches damaged. This day I was starting back to Shanghai after an orphanage visitation with my student, Marie, as passenger. Father Claasen strode across to the car and asked if I would give two missionary priests a lift back to Shanghai. Of course I would, and they got into the back seat.

The day was brilliantly sunny without being hot, for we had just had a day and night of torrential rain. During the night a single flash of lightning would light up the buildings and yard as clearly as day for what seemed to be a full minute. As I feared, the heavy rain had made muddy ruts in the road. When we were far into the countryside, I saw the road ahead had been washed away completely over a ravine.

For the length of a car, the divide opened over a very deep ditch. However, someone had driven that same road ahead of us and had improvised a strange bridge. Across the broken road we saw a flat plank or board to accommodate the wheels on one side of a car. For the other side of the car, the driver had laid a slice of corrugated pipe, or so it looked. It was not completely flattened, but the sides slightly curved, indicating the pipe had either been cut lengthwise or was old and worn.

I stopped the jeep and my passengers got out, as I did, to examine this bridge. We walked across to the other side. I was not encouraged when I noticed all my passengers stayed there. I went back to the car alone and got in. The missionaries moved the plank and the pipe to line them up with my wheels. Then they stood back to direct traffic—me. To my dismay, relying as I was on their directions, they and Marie all motioned in different directions. A great wisdom descended on me. I told myself to remember this in all situations hereafter when people were trying to direct me. I could only rely on myself—and God. So I looked away from them, made a big sign of the Cross on myself, and stepped on the gas. And suddenly, I was across, I was safe, I was alive. About then my knees turned to jelly.

I didn't realize how unusual it was in Shanghai to see a woman driving a jeep or any other car. When driving I wore my gray beret, not my veiled hat. The jeep was wide open and the beret was more practical than wind-blown veil or hair. I remember one small incident. Perhaps dark descended early, as in winter or fall, but certainly it was dark when I stopped at the red light. We did not usually see many soldiers in the city, so I noticed a scattered number of uniformed men in the street. Suddenly a soldier jumped up into the seat alongside of me, shoving me to the right. In a flash I saw that he was small and slight, so I just shoved him back and, to my amazement, he slid to the ground. I drove off. I always remembered that I had no emotional reaction to the little episode, neither alarm nor fear. It simply was a happening.

When I applied for my driver's license, I learned that I must have a Chinese name and a *chop* (stamp). Rowena took the matter in hand and prompted me in choosing a name. Most of us whose last names began with Mac or Mc were given a choice of a word with the phonetic sound of that first syllable. Father McGoey, for example, chose Mi, pronounced Mee, meaning rice in Mandarin. I chose Mei, pronounced May, meaning wheat. The person who would make the ivory chop and engrave it with my name then searched the classic poems for a fitting combination of three words from a line of poetry. Mine came out Mei Lan Shang, translated Wheat Iris Fragrance. In tiny black characters on the white side of the chop was the name of the engraver. I could know my stamped signature had no duplicate in China. This has become my treasured souvenir of those days of wind and moon.

The jeep had been donated for use in our work, of course, but since everything we did was under that category, we used it constantly. Much as I had enjoyed the leisurely pedicab rides, leisure was not my priority when there was so much to be done in what seemed so little time. I found out from the Fathers how to get my license, learned that I could or could not (I forget which) turn right on a red light, and noted that many, if not most, of the traffic cops were tall, turbaned Sikhs with black beards.

Another American sister in Shanghai belonged to the Good Shepherd congregation. These were cloistered nuns, dedicated to caring for girls from unfortunate backgrounds. Sister Mary (I shall call her) was a young nun permitted to leave the cloister during the day to shop for the groceries and other necessities. She spoke Chinese fluently and had been a missionary here for at least five years. Until now, she had done all the shopping in a pedicab or ricksha. But at last someone had donated a small van to the convent.

Now that I was driving a jeep around town, the Good Shepherd Superior asked if I would teach Sister Mary to drive. Why, of course I would.

Our first lesson was the last. Since her van had the same gear shift as my jeep, we took the jeep, and I drove to a quiet, flat stretch of road near Ming Hong, the red brick mental hospital run by the Maryknoll Brothers. Sister Mary took my place at the wheel and we began, after a few explanations from me, to move forward. I had explained the brake, the clutch and gears to her, but she had only begun to roll, hands on wheel, when into our path stepped a tall Chinese pushing a wheelbarrow. He came from the side of the road and deliberately walked just ahead of our vehicle.

Reaching for the wheel I steered left to avoid the man. But he was very quick. I hand-braked the jeep to a halt, but not before the man had thrown himself directly in front of our car. I don't know how Sister Mary and I changed places so fast, but I was at the wheel when a hand like steel clamped on my forearm. I had no idea where this second man came from. Evidently, he had been close by. He began shouting at me in Chinese, probably saying I had killed his dearest friend, who now lay under our wheels. This was not at all true. The wheels never touched him. Sister Mary shouted right back at our accuser. She told him to put his friend in the back seat and we would take him to the hospital. While he was getting the man onto his feet, totally unhurt, and into the back seat, Sister Mary said, "Money! That's all they want. We didn't touch the man."

At the hospital our victim lay groaning, bent over as if in great pain. A nurse examined him right there on the floor, found nothing, not even a scratch, and said so. I used the office phone to call Father McGoey, who came immediately to the rescue with a pocketful of Chinese money and a few Chinese words, well-chosen, I was sure. The man pocketed the money and walked out of the door with all the injured dignity he could muster. Father McGoey laughed with amusement at the entire episode, suggesting that he would have bet something like this was bound to happen and that two nuns on a lonely road should know they were easy marks for such shenanigans. The men were farmers, not thugs, and just wanted a little ready *kumshaw*, about all they would get from the likes of us. He then offered to teach Sister Mary himself or get one of the brothers to do it.

—9—

Where Can I Find a Rest Room?

At this point, I should bring up the matter of rest rooms. After daylong journeys by bus, train or jeep, the nonexistence of rest room stops presented a real problem. On such journeys, the men relieved themselves publicly without self-consciousness. One of my students told me that the men took for granted no polite person would look at them. What women did, I never knew. A double standard of modesty seemed to prevail. No provision was made for women's comfort or privacy. Were we supposed to have been made of more refined clay?

And speaking of that, as a nun, I had a long tradition behind me of what I might call "ethereality," which is to say, being not of this earth. Many orders of women religious were forbidden by their rule of life to eat with laypeople. I think the idea was that our act of eating would disedify the laity, who liked to think of us as either too spiritual to feel hunger or too spiritual to satisfy such earthbound pangs. If, then, to see us eat breakfast, lunch or dinner might disillusion a lay Catholic, what would happen to his or her faith if we excused ourselves and went to the rest room? These were the inhibiting thoughts in my mind.

I recall the day of my deepest embarrassment. I was to revisit the orphanage at Ningpo, an overnight trip by steamer as recounted earlier. We had shipped the sisters a huge crate of diapers and canned milk for the infants and I wanted to make sure the Chinese personnel (old orphans mainly) were well instructed in hygienic preparation of the formula. I had seen flies inside of nippled bottles with babies nursing. I was taking Marie as my interpreter, with full instructions to teach the crêche staff something about flies not being proper flavoring for babies' milk.

Our boat arrived before five o'clock in the morning. As we disembarked, we saw posted signs forbidding us to return to the boat for any reason whatsoever. Marie and I found our way to the church, where we attended the 5:30 Mass. I thought perhaps the pastor would ask us in for coffee, helping us to kill time. But this did not happen. We wandered into the street to look for something that would pass for tea, coffee or breakfast. All we found was a warm coke at a vegetable stand. We still had until nine o'clock, about three hours, before the sisters would expect us at the orphanage.

Thoughts of home and bathroom began to creep into my mind willy-nilly. Primly aware of venturing on dangerous ground in the presence of a layperson, a good Catholic girl, I mentioned to Marie that I wondered if there was any place.... I let the thought trail, but I had made my point. She looked very embarrassed, but said her aunt lived in town. We could go there. I brightened. We called a ricksha at once.

Over the cobblestones we jostled and jogged for an interminable distance, it seemed to me. But at last we arrived at a nice two-story Chinese house, closely bordered by neighbors' homes. We were welcomed joyously by what appeared to be dozens of relatives of all sizes, shapes and ages. We were brought into a central room. In came neighbors, excited and pleased to see little Marie, the college girl niece, and to meet her friend and teacher. A Catholic sister? Many of them were Catholic, I learned, and they were very curious about what I was wearing—the gray hat, the veil, the uniform, the medal of the Dove, emblem of the Holy Spirit.

I nudged Marie when I could get near her through the crowded room. "Marie, ask your aunt...." She knew what I meant and nodded. I saw her whisper in her aunt's ear. A startled blank expression swiftly passed over the lady's face to become a look of inspired decision. She nodded and left the room. At last! I knew she would lead me to a haven of privacy.

Not so. Into the crowd came two young men. One carried two screens, the other, a commode, which they set in the very center of the room, stationing the screens around it. When they left, the aunt took my limp arm and led me like a lamb to the guillotine. She gently pushed me inside the screen, where I stood contemplating the commode "in uffish thought," my inhibitions screaming. When I thought I had stood there an appropriate length of time, I came out. Everyone smiled at me happily. I forced my way through the throng to Marie, who was standing beside her aunt.

"Oh dear, we are already late," I said. "We must go." Marie somehow commandeered a ricksha and we were off, waving goodbye. Again we jostled and jolted over cobblestones, arrived at the orphanage where, the Lord be praised, whatever the language, everyone knew the secret code: W.C.

I think it was after this trip that when I returned to Shanghai I found enormous posters of Stalin displayed in the windows of all big department stores. His arms were outstretched, he smiled benevolently. His printed words were, "Come home, my children." It was the White Russians he meant. I found my Russian staff excited and restless. I knew they were faced with decision. To go or not to go. The promise he gave was of homes, jobs, security. Ships were already in the harbor to take them home to Mother Russia.

—10—

Moon Festival Time— We Move Into Our Own Home

Sister Candida never forgot for a moment that we needed a convent of our own. At last she learned of an attractive Western-style two-story house in the French concession. It was across the street and down the block from the Russian Orthodox Church. The owner was a high official in the Nanking government. We both fell in love with the house, and Candida had the extraordinary good fortune to be introduced by a mutual friend to the owner's wife. He was willing to sell, she said, for a very good price if paid in U.S. currency.

Sister and I were faced with a dilemma. Chiang Kai-shek had just issued a proclamation stating that anyone dealing in the black market would be shot. Sister and I did not aspire to such an end. I didn't attend Candida's meeting with the owner's wife, for my command of Chinese was extremely limited and I wanted Candida to use all her powers of persuasion uninhibited by my foreign presence. She told me that she used every argument against payment in U.S. dollars, even to shaming the woman as wife of a high government official for attempting to break the law. Candida and I remembered, too, that our Society expressly taught us never to break the laws of any country where we might serve.

Finally came a day of complete deadlock when both

parties agreed to sleep over the matter. Candida and I prayed together and again the next morning at Mass. After breakfast, she went out to deliver our unwavering answer: No purchase in U.S. dollars. We knew the house was lost to us.

But it was not. When she returned at lunchtime, her face was shining, her brown eyes sparkled. The house was ours. The owner had capitulated. How the financing would be handled was not our responsibility. All would be taken care of through the Los Angeles Motherhouse and Sister Frederica's advisors in Shanghai. We were tremendously relieved and happy to have our own place at last. As Candida's letter relates, family and friends would help us furnish the place piece by piece. The cases holding big items like the refrigerator, donated by Mrs. James McClatchy of Sacramento, gave wood for hand-made furniture. And to guard our home, we had Rex, the German shepherd, given us by a departing White Russian family.

An excerpt from Candida's letter home follows:

...Last week I gave my mother's group a tea in the convent. Believe it or not, I made the cakes, the cookies, the sandwiches all by myself. The reason was twofold. First of all to thank them for the work they are doing for us—of course, for God—then to thank them for the donation many of them in this group had given for the beautiful table—could be used as an altar—and also to let them see many things we still need in the house. My only disappointment was half of them didn't show up, for it was the feast of St. Stanislaus, who is very popular with the Chinese gentlemen as their patron saint, so these ladies' fathers, husbands or uncles have him for their name day. They have their own party at home. It is a beautiful thought to think that they, too, celebrate their feast days. On this coming Wednesday I will start a new club with teenage girls. Most of them are Catholics, good fervent pious girls. So we must pray hard that they will see and listen to the inspiration of the Holy Spirit (as possible vocations). I am having these clubs—the choir and the Girls' Club—in the convent, for in the afternoon I have private lessons and I can't make it from one place to another. My club begins at 1:30 and lasts till 3:00, then right away from 3:00 to 5:00 I give English lessons.

Of course I arrange my schedule such that on those days when I have club meetings and classes, I am not cook on that day. Father Gatz has found us here in our new address and has given me several cases for counseling. I am going to teach two ladies on Friday and my English classes, so the day is quite short for me. I save all my morning for visiting, office work, interviews, etc. It is fun isn't it, to race with the day. I prefer much, much more to run a race than to lie in bed waiting for the time to pass away.

I shall be most grateful if you Groupwork Sisters could give me some idea how to make decorations for the Christmas tree with papers, etc. (Not too expensive to get. Always have China in mind when you make those samples.) I have some balls and trees made of paper from Sister Joan, but I need more. No, popcorns are too expensive and so are candies to put on the tree, something with color paper will be more practical.

To all the dear Sisters who wrote us we thank you, please do continue your acts of charity.

At this point I add my own letter home, which gives further insight into our daily life:

Moon Festival Time

Shanghai, September 25, 1947

Dearest Sisters Everywhere:

And so last night we put our Community's picture on our little dining room table, leaning against our Lady's image, with a big yellow iris shining behind you both. This is the season of the Moon Festival, so one eats moon cakes that are like little pies filled with fragrant lotus seeds or watermelon seeds and other fruit or coconut. Don't you know about the lady living in the moon palace and the rabbit that is cooking something good and it gives you long life? The moon is so brilliant these nights—for the Moon Festival, of course. Candida says people must give each other gifts at this season—and PAY BILLS. There are four times a year one pays bills. And here I thought every month I must—one pays bills on the New Year, on the Dragon Festival, the Moon Festival—and when is the other one?

The cost of living is soaring now—one egg, 1,500 CNC (Chinese National Currency)—one orange, 8,000 CNC—bread, 5,000 CNC at cheapest. The dollar is 60,000 CNC today! Indeed China needs a collector at home. Much as I would hate to leave China—for now I am working hard on learning Mandarin, and I see very well the needs and problems—nothing can be done here if we cannot support the work and the sisters. I would collect gladly in the States. The poor U.S.! Well, the generosity of America should save her soul.

I told you about the weather of Shanghai in summertime. Now it is delightful—no, not today, for a typhoon wind is driving us crazy—but for the most part it has been ideal. We are well established in our own house now and love it! We need more gray uniforms running, I mean walking, around in it. We have a German police dog, given by a Russian family on their way back to Russia, the land of milk, honey and St.

Stalin. I was sick to hear the four-year-old child of this good Catholic couple tell me with great pride that she was going, not to Russia, but to *Soviet* Russia—and see Father Stalin! The mother said she does not know where she learned to speak that way; but of course, from family friends.

Thousands are leaving weekly now. We are right across from the Soviet Church, did I tell you? About the dog, I mean His Majesty, Rex! He is such a playful puppy, in love with everyone who comes. He greets them joyfully by leaping to his full height of almost—well, he can knock a man down with one bat of his paw—and when the visitor, be he carpenter or bishop, sees that mouthful of teeth laughing at eye-level in his face, it is all he can do to keep from fleeing. At night Rex barks gloriously, by far the loudest and most fearsome bellow on the street. And to him it is all in fun. A burglar would be so welcome, like a playfellow in his simple way of thinking. They say he will grow some more! Let us start an album of Community dogs the world over! With a biography and character sketch of each.

The Bishop came to see us. Sister Candida was on vacation at her family's, so Rex and I received him. He looks like St. Nicholas and is just as kind and fatherly. He said we must have a chapel right away and Mass and the Blessed Sacrament reserved. He will lend us everything until we can get our own.

We have had the carpenter here providing us with shelves to put things on. Kitchen, pantry and linen-cabinet—all fixed. We feel so right; really we have very much now, with what Sister Lucile sent us! I feel guilty having a Frigidaire when I have seen hospitals that do not have one. By the way, do you know anyone who would send a portable phonograph (not electric) to the Wuhu mission? It would help so much there. I promised to ask—maybe a club would like to adopt this mission run by Spanish Fathers. Any bids? They need money mostly, but also various things.

Sister Candida ends her vacation this week. So do I. On my feast day her sister asked me to their house for tea. I am wise now and know that *tea* means you won't need any supper after. And they had ice cream and cake for me—an American touch. Two girls played the violin and piano later—it was all so very pleasant.

Next door we have a school, so balls come flying over the trees along our fence continually. We have finally trained the boys to know that it is a great misfortune to lose the balls in that way; for they won't get them back until the next day. And now that we have Rex, they do not get them at all if he gets them first.

China is so beautiful—everything is simplified here, slowed down, and the rhythm of life is languid, tranquil, unruffled. At first it bothers you. Pretty soon, you see the wisdom in it. You see that the climate has much to do with it and that the people have learned how to live in China. If we are to live here we, too, must learn how to live, how to eat, how to rest, or we cannot work here for the Lord. China will eat you, someone told me, if you do not eat well; for there is small nourishment in the food. In summertime everyone stops working and plans only to exist—great wisdom born of experience. In winter, everyone endures the cold and learns to love the sun. They learn also how to make the bed. Chinese girls roll up in their bedding and are perfectly warm. They know how to dress for the cold too. That is what strikes me here—how important it becomes to everyone to survive at all. The work is important, yes, very, but a dead man does not get much done. Pretty soon you also are simplified and you see in your social work that, for a long time, simple relief problems must be the bulk of your case load. The people have few emotional problems while they are absorbed in the one thought—how to live through this season?

The one newspaper we see daily is anti-American and reflects the feeling of Shanghailanders, especially of the merchant class and on down. The government is now arresting factory workers for communistic affiliations, and this will either succeed in suppressing Communism (not likely) or it will bring out of hiding the Shanghai Communists. So far, the students are the only Communists in the big cities to demonstrate. The rest of the Communists are not known or else they are in the army fighting outside the cities. All the wars you hear about are in the country places; small towns are taken, not cities, even though they come within 20 miles of Peking, for example. They confine their activities to sabotage of communication lines between the city and China. Life goes on just as if the wars were in America and not in our own land. China is used to this fighting business and just disregards it totally—like a sleepy man who has a fly buzzing around has face and he is too tired to swat it—until one day he feels its bite; then he strikes. Now the government is striking because communistic turmoil prevents the U.S. from giving aid.

Pray for us—we know you do! And without your being right there in back of us, holding us up like a strong wall, I don't know what we'd do. Funny, the States seem very near. China used to seem across the world when I looked at the horizon in the west—but now when I look at the eastern horizon I see all of you lined up on the shore, with the veils blowing in the winds, and it is very, very near to China.

Lovingly in the Holy Spirit,
Sister Mariel

–11–

The Russian Disconnection

My Russian staff had carried on the agency's function efficiently, imaginatively and with zeal. They had even extended service to people outside the Russian community. When a Polish woman was referred to the Russian office by Father Wilcox, I decided to visit her myself to show my personal interest. Anya accompanied me, and we found the address on a street lined with two- and three-story framed houses, reminiscent of crowded San Francisco apartments at the turn of the century. A short flight of wooden steps led to a front door left slightly ajar by the last person to enter.

A Chinese family lived here, and the Polish woman, whom I shall call Sophia, had been able to rent a space under the staircase. I remember we pushed open the door and found ourselves in a windowless hallway. How the cavernous space under the staircase, directly in front of us, was lighted I do not know. But lighted it was, and we saw it on entering much like a stage setting, lit for the play to begin. At the right, a narrow staircase began its winding ascent to what I knew were the individual apartments and rooms of family members, as I had seen in Candida's family home. In the lighted cavern beneath the stairs stood a huge single bed, piled high with bedding or whatever else served for warmth. At the head of the bed sat, upright, a white-haired woman, very fair-skinned and extremely thin and wrinkled.

A few steps took us to her bedside, and she welcomed us gratefully. Her English was excellent, and Anya quickly learned she spoke fluent Russian as well. How she came to China and how she came to be in this sorry state of solitude and affliction she told us briefly. Stricken as she was with tuberculosis, with scarce food and no medication, she could not talk long without coughing and otherwise losing breath.

I judged her, at first glance, to be about sixty-five. I learned she was my own age, thirty-six. From her manner and speech, she was obviously of the elite class in her home town, probably on the border of Poland and Russia. Her hair turned white, she told us, on the night she saw her husband, father and brother shot dead before her eyes. This reasonably may have happened in 1941, when Russians invaded Poland and ruthlessly killed intellectuals as well as property owners. Passing for Russian, she escaped to Moscow with other refugees. Thousands fled. The Trans-Siberian Railway would have taken her to the northern border of China and Manchuria in nine days. China was the only country to open its arms to the White Russians, among whom Sophia had doubtless cast her lot, and with them she would have found harbor in Harbin. How she came to Shanghai and to a Chinese home, rather than to a Russian household, I did not ask. Perhaps she was able to buy her way with the Chinese and did not make close friends with the Russians. It is only perhaps. I did notice, as time went on, that although my Russian girls supplied her with food and clothing and did what they could to get her medical aid, they did not give her the individual warm and caring attention I expected of them. She was an outsider, even though stateless, as they were.

With strong, insistent propaganda still hammering at the White Russian community, I found Ludmila, Anya, Kristina and Catherine anxious and extremely disturbed. Ludmila said her mother wanted to "go home to Russia." Catherine, the stronger willed of the two sisters, had already made up her mind. "After all," she said, "it is my motherland. My roots are there. Why would I not want to go back?" Ludmila said very little. I was to remember that later.

I was to remember it because of what happened, and I may as well tell it at this juncture, without concern for the actual sequence of events.

The Stalin outreach occurred at the beginning of Shanghai's hot summer. July and August, I recall, were brutally hot and a foreigner like myself felt its full impact. I remember it was hard to slake thirst with tepid, boiled water. Ice or ice-cold water was only something to dream about. One day I cast caution to the winds and drank water from the tap. Not long after, of course, I was in sore straits and agreed to a short stay in the hospital. My Eurasian woman doctor extended the stay by a week or two as an enforced rest. Ambulatory as I was, I strolled along the hallway one morning toward a sun porch where I planned to sit awhile and read. To my surprise, I met Sophia, the Polish woman, and quickly felt hostility. I was happy that she was here in the hospital, thinking that Anya had arranged for her admission. But her first words told me Anya had nothing to do with her presence here.

"Why did your agency drop me?" she said accusingly. "For a week they brought me nothing. I got up out of bed and walked to your office. The sign had been changed to 'Soviet Only.' Why did you change to Soviet only?" she demanded angrily.

I assured her I had no idea that this had happened, but she turned abruptly and limped away.

As soon as I was released, I went to the office. It was locked. The sign was gone, both the original and the other. No sign of the staff, no sign of relief goods remained. I learned from Father Wilcox that they had sailed. Catherine had told me she would go and "I will be put to work in a factory," she had said "and with every pull of my arm and muscle I will pray for my country, for my homeland."

Kristina may have sailed to another country, for she had talked of Canada, of Australia, of America. But I never saw her again. I knew Ludmila returned to Russia and assumed that Anya did also. I never blamed them for their sudden disappearance or anything they did regarding the agency. Survival was the name of the game, and none of us know what we would do when the chips are down.

-12-

What to Do About Lillian?

It may have been as early as April when Lillian was left on my doorstep, so to speak. I had returned from a visit to the Kashing orphanage, fifty miles north of Shanghai, run by the Cabrini Sisters. This orphanage stays in my memory for the story of its bombing. In the foyer of the crèche I saw a statue of Mary often seen on holy cards. Her arms are outstretched, and her feet stand on a huge serpent, representing the devil. I could see the statue was perfectly intact, except for the head of the serpent. The crèche had been bombed, they told me, perhaps by Japanese during one war or another. The babies had all been removed before the bombing but the building had been totally demolished. Only this statue of Mary still stood, untouched except for the blasted head of the serpent.

On arrival home from this trip I went to my office to write a report. Rowena, my Chinese office manager, came to tell me I was needed below. On my way downstairs to our lower offices, she filled me in. A Eurasian girl about twelve years old had been brought to the office by the pastor of St. Peter's Church.

"Father asks us to find her a home," Rowena explained, adding, "Her name is Lillian. She has an aunt but no parents."

I knew this was my case, not my students' responsibility, for the girl was clearly not Chinese. She was a small, dark-haired, pretty child who looked even younger than twelve. Candida told me later she had learned from the pastor that the aunt was a prostitute. She had taken care of Lillian when the child was apparently orphaned. I needed to talk with this aunt. Through the pastor, we were able to get word to her to see me at the office.

Meanwhile, Lillian had run away from home and refused to return to her aunt. She had sought refuge on the doorstep of St. Peter's rectory that morning. The pastor had turned to us for an answer to the question, "Where is this child to sleep tonight and, for that matter, every night?"

I was to find that Lillian, who looked like a quiet, well-mannered little girl with no aspiration to be more grown up than her age, was not wanted in any Catholic school in town. She had been enrolled in all of them and had the reputation of being a trouble-maker par excellence. I was told by principals and teachers that she stole, she lied, she cheated, she led others into every school-oriented iniquity. No school would take her back. Meanwhile, her aunt persuaded her to return on condition that we find another home, another school, another solution.

Since the aunt was a prostitute, her home was obviously not the environment for a child. So we pushed on in our search and finally found an army officer's wife who would take Lillian as a helper in the household. I breathed a sigh of relief. It was not the best, for her schooling stopped. But for the moment it must do.

Lillian's aunt was a gaunt, fairly tall black-haired woman whose face was always powdered chalk white and cheekbones roundly rouged. She held her hand, always gloved in white, in front of her mouth, explaining she had a facial injury that caused either a tic or an unsightly and fixed grimace of which she was ashamed. Her head slightly shook, as if palsied. If she gave Rowena her name initially, I never really grasped what it was and knew her only as Lillian's aunt.

I had taught my social work class the importance of

keeping records. Rowena, bless her, faithfully recorded every contact we had with Lillian and her aunt, and this was to prove extremely helpful at a future date. For Lillian did not last long at the army officer's home. She was caught red-handed stealing jewelry. Once more I found her waiting for me in the office. By this time, I had exhausted every school and childcare institution in the area. She had told me that the place she had been happiest was with the Maryknoll Sisters at Ming Hong, the mental hospital. The sisters lived near this hospital, operated by the Maryknoll Brothers. I contacted the administrative brother and told him Lillian wished to live with the sisters as she had before. However, he regretfully refused without giving me what I considered a valid reason.

At my wit's end, I went to the Bishop. Without appointment, I was lucky to find him free to give me a half-hour of his time. I left Lillian in the jeep while I explained the situation—an orphaned twelve-year-old girl, a child refused by every Catholic institution, a child who had a prostitute for a guardian. The Bishop shook his head in pity for the girl, but had no solution. I played my trump. I excused myself and went to the jeep. I brought Lillian before the Bishop.

"Where is this child to sleep tonight, Your Excellency?" I asked.

He looked a bit startled, as if he realized I might intend to leave her right there on that very spot. I repeated the child's wish to live again with the Maryknoll Sisters at Ming Hong, where she had been, they told me, a great help with many chores. The sisters evidently took care of the laundry, ironing, and meals for the patients in the mental hospital.

"If you request it," I urged, "I am sure the brothers will consent."

And so it was arranged. Without further ado, the Bishop called the brothers on the phone. Lillian happily returned to the sisters at Ming Hong and, for once, was received with love and appreciation. I thought the case was closed, as did Rowena, who filed away the record she had faithfully kept.

Months passed. I will skip over these months for the moment in order to wrap up the story of Lillian in my life.

One day between travels I was going through mail and cleaning out my desk at the office when I noticed an unsealed folded paper covered with red and black Chinese characters. I thought it must be an ad of some sort and threw it in the wastebasket, where it lay for a day or two before I discovered I had tossed out a summons to court. I was being sued.

Rowena found the summons and told me I was to appear before the court on a given day at a specified hour. Lillian's aunt accused me of knowingly placing her niece in a mental hospital because the child was pregnant.

Lillian was pregnant? How could that be? With Rowena's help, I hired a lawyer, who accompanied the two of us to Ming Hong for a talk with Lillian. She made a sworn statement to the effect that I had no knowledge of her pregnancy at any time. She said that while she lived with the army officer and his wife, the houseboy had taken advantage of her on several occasions. She had not told anyone until her pregnancy became evident. Then she told the sisters, who informed her aunt. The nuns truly loved the girl and insisted on her remaining with them. This the aunt was glad to allow.

It so turned out that my Chinese lawyer had to be in Nanking the day of my court hearing. With Rowena's airtight records of the case and Lillian's affidavit, I felt I would not need a lawyer as much as I needed my own interpreter. For this I chose Rowena.

When we came into the courtroom, my accuser and I took our places behind podiums that faced a two-layered panel of judges, seated in rows, one above the other.

Rowena took her place at my left and the court interpreter stood beside Lillian's aunt. Before anyone spoke, Rowena handed the judge our records of the case. I don't know what a British courtroom looks like, but I had the distinct impression I was in an English court of law, although no one wore a white wig.

Rowena showed complete poise. Although I had the feeling that everyone on the panel understood English perfectly, the entire proceedings were conducted in Chinese. Through the court interpreter the judge questioned Lillian's aunt.

My accuser, with her trembling head and her white-gloved hand hiding her mouth, did not impress the jury well. Neither did her occupation. I, on the other hand, had everything going for me. And Rowena was a superb Portia in my defense. However, I had been told by my employers and other foreign allies that if my accuser had been Chinese and not herself a foreigner, all I thought I had going for me might not have been enough. As it was, the case was dismissed.

So ended my contact with Lillian and her aunt. In due time, we learned that her baby was a boy whom she named Freddie. Under the care of the Maryknoll Sisters, mother and child were all right, I knew. What became of them after Mao's army marched in, I will never know.

–13–

1947 *Draws to a Close*

November 1947 was for both Candida and me the ending of a chapter. We waited impatiently for the page to be turned by the arrival of more sisters to join us around the little kitchen table we used for meals as much as for chopping vegetables. Mrs. Wong, one of Candida's volunteers, shopped for us. Grocers thought it bad luck to sell their wares to nuns or Buddhist monks. Why? Candida explained that we were not living the usual, normal life and so were suspect and they were not taking any chances on luck.

A full year since our arrival in China, we were settled in our work and had a convent home prepared to welcome the expected reinforcements.

We were enjoying our house, large yard and faithful German shepherd guardian more and more. The yard was contained by a high bamboo fence that separated us on one side from an elementary school. We were serenaded throughout the morning hours by children shouting their lessons at the top of their voices in unison. At recess, the boys and girls peeked through the bamboo fence posts, teasing Rex however they could. He knew they were up to no good and rushed at the fence, barking angrily. We confined him to the other side of the house or indoors at such times. A gentle, affectionate dog, he took a dislike to children for their teasing, and we were afraid he would nip one of them if he got a chance. Actually, the only person he ever tried to bite was the school principal, who, for some reason, dropped in at the convent. Fortunately we restrained Rex in time.

Our chapel meant very much to us. Candida's sewing club and friends had donated a beautiful black teakwood table for an altar. Father Valerian, a Franciscan, came daily to offer Mass. I remember his favorite expression was "e-e-easy does it." He said Mass for us at dawn, wearing paper-thin vestments over his light summer suit. Our own uniforms were often damp with perspiration when the half-hour Mass ended. I learned to love the little hand-held fan, used by men and women alike, without which the Shanghai summer would have had no survivors.

Our work had settled down by autumn's transition into winter's outer fringe. With the Russians gone that agency was closed. Rowena still managed the Chinese office with the aid of volunteers. I continued work for the CWCC, but travel between cities was not the open thing it had been. Visas were suddenly required from city to city, indicating political troubles of which I knew nothing. I know now what the government knew then. Communists were destroying the railway line both north and south of Mukden. This linked together the two base areas that lay in the path of the strategic Peking-Hankow railway.

As for Candida, she had returned to China after ten years, a mature young woman, trained and experienced in the dedicated life of her vocation. This religious commitment set her somewhat apart from former friends as well as the lay people she worked with now. She had become a role model, a counselor, a friend on a pedestal. This can be a lonely place. Her personality and warm outreach to others had attracted several young women to consider following the vocation she represented, just as she attracted boys and girls of the parish community in the clubs she organized. Her work was in full swing and I could see by her sparkling brown eyes and ready smile that she felt fulfilled in her work.

Suddenly the wait was over. Early in December we

received a wire from Sister Frederica, directing us to meet a Pan American flight on December tenth, bearing Sisters Alice and Lucile. The third member of the expected trio, Sister Magdolna, would arrive a week later on the SS *Marine Swallow*.

The plane was due about three on a cold, gray December afternoon. We were sorry the new sisters would miss seeing the reds and golds of Shanghai's spreading oaks and elms in autumnal glory. November chill had now given way to December frosts, and the streets were lined only with the bare silver bones of tree trunks and limbs. We took the jeep and drove to the airfield in plenty of time to scan the skies and listen for the drone of the engines for nearly an hour. We didn't talk. We were cloaked in the privacy of our own thoughts. Relief, relief, relief filled us both, each of us for different reasons. I was glad to turn over the responsibility to our arriving head, Sister Alice Slachta. Candida exulted, I knew, in the fulfillment of her dream, now to be realized. Sister Alice would be empowered to open the novitiate training for young women.

When at last we heard and saw the silver plane, our emotions took off—and, apparently, so did we. Sister Lucile described in a letter home what she saw from the window looking down on the airfield:

"I saw, first, two gray uniforms. When they caught sight of our waving handkerchiefs, Sisters Mariel and Candida began jumping up and down, waving back. Then they broke all the rules of the airport by breaking through the barrier and running right out into the field...."

Yes, I suppose we did, for we were hugging the two and walking back to the building, locating the luggage and loading it and our sisters into the jeep—all in a blur of excited, glad chatter and potpourri of emotions. Candida's ever-ready tears flowed for joy.

We were gratified to see the surprised pleasure in the eyes of the faces of the sisters as we approached our pretty house and entered the basement garage. Dog Rex barked happily in greeting, watching from the fenced yard until we could introduce him properly. We had prepared the largest rooms upstairs for the four of us when Magdolna would arrive and a downstairs room for our Superior, Sister Alice.

The floors, though bare of rugs or carpeting, were polished hardwood throughout the house, and I could see Alice and Lucile assessing each room for what was needed in drapes and furniture to make the place home. The modern bathroom, with tub but no shower, pleased them. The kitchen was poorly equipped by U.S. standards in spite of the American refrigerator. The sink had begun leaking through a rusted, cracked pipe that led from sink to an outlet in the floorboards. I had therefore strung empty tin cans along the pipe for protective covering. It worked pretty well but amused Lucile no end. Alice clucked her tongue and shook her head, and I knew something would be done soon to displace my attempted maintenance. Pipes ran above our heads the length of the ceiling. I warned them that if you entered the kitchen at night you would see a rat walking the pipe. (This situation did not change. We accepted and lived with things in China's post-war conditions, as did everyone else.)

Candida and I were naturally intensely interested in gauging the personality of our new Superior. Sister Alice was not tall, about five-foot-two and compactly built but not heavy. She had very fair skin, blue eyes, and wore her gray hair brushed back in a bun. Her manner was not overly mothering. While she had a concerned eye for needs, health and welfare, she made us feel we were all adults together and she, at fifty-three, was our older sister. She spoke English very well, and she took hold of the house and her responsibilities immediately. We liked her.

Less than a week after the first two arrivals, Lucile drove the jeep to the dock to meet Magdolna. Lucile went alone, since the disembarking would be long and the rest of us were needed at home or at our jobs. The biting cold numbed her hands and feet during the hours she watched the anchored ship. She suffered frostbite that day from which she never fully recovered. When the long wait ended and she brought the Hungarian sister home, we were surprised on two counts. First, Magdolna could speak only a hesitant word or two of English. I had supposed she would speak as fluently as Sister Alice. The second surprise was to hear Lucile speak more than a word or two of Hungarian, a great blessing for Magdolna. Lucile would be able to teach her English.

Lucile explained how she had picked up a bit of Hungarian. I knew that she had been the first American girl to enter the SSS community, but I had not known that she and a second sister had been sent to Budapest to spend part of their training at the Motherhouse. From the foundress herself, Sister Margaret Slachta, they were able to imbibe the spirit and vision she desired for this newly created religious society. Lucile learned from the example of the foundress and other sisters spiritually formed by her, what the sister herself was to be like. She was to be a joyously free spirit, of that I was sure, for I had learned from Luciles's own example.

Magdolna was a young nurse. She was extremely thin, with large brown eyes that reflected, it seemed to me, the tragedy of life in wartime Europe. Both she and Alice had come from a time we could not fully imagine, and Magdolna's drawn face told a sad story. However, her smile was quickly responsive to all we were doing and Alice assigned her to creating much that was lovely in both our house and our routine home life. She sewed a beautiful backdrop for our altar and chapel sanctuary, she took over the household chores of cooking and laundering, while learning English from Lucile. Eventually she would be nursing in a hospital at some mission, but she must learn Chinese first.

Lucile, in her first letter to the Motherhouse, wrote the following:

> The twenty-fourth was a busy, busy day. We all worked everywhere, doing everything, joining each other, helping each other just to get done for midnight Mass. I had my first experience with a pedicab, as Sister Alice asked me to go downtown shopping for her, and also to get the necessary provisions. That was something—riding on a pedicab—I'll never forget it as long as I live. I felt a mixture of an air of distinction, mingled with amusement and an occasional gulp of apprehension for my safety.... I did all the required shopping, spent thousands and thousands of Chinese money, all told, about twelve dollars in American money, and came home loaded, both my pockets and the pedicab. People kept coming in to pay respects and bringing gifts, and Sister Alice and I were trying to get the baking done for the open house for the priests on the twenty-sixth and the nuns on the twenty-eighth, besides trying to get the house in order, run errands and get our gray veils ready by midnight and have our own Christmas party. Well, everything was in readiness, by postponing our Christmas party until Christmas Day...we put the last stitch on our veils just as Father Valerian rang the gate bell. Midnight Mass followed.

Representatives of all local religious orders, such as Jesuits, Franciscans and Greek Catholics came, as did missionaries passing through. The same was true of the nuns. All were interested in and curious about the new sisters who didn't wear traditional garb, went about singly, not in pairs, drove cars, and worked directly among the people, not in institutions. We served cookies, cakes, sandwiches and lemonade, Coca-Cola, coffee and tea. We sang Christmas carols, each in his/her own tongue, but in unison. And with Lucile as emcee, her brown eyes shining, everyone had a rousing good time. Group workers that Candida and I were, long practiced in children's games, we suggested and Lucile, with her strong melodious voice, led rounds with somewhat silly words. Everyone laughed at the translations if they didn't speak English, and sang anyway.

—14—

1948 Begins

The new year brought January's knife-sharp cold, which we fended off inside the house with fire in our coke-burning stove. Both wood and coke were purchased by Mrs. Wong and Candida together, for one paid for these necessities by weight, and it didn't take a trained eye to see that the vendors soaked the wood in water to add weight. I think Candida's presence and sharp bargaining know-how supported Mrs. Wong's in the dim hope of intimidating the vendor into a modicum of honesty.

Early in the new year, Mother Thornton, the Dean of Studies, invited Sister Lucile to take over my classes in social work, with the addition of one or two other courses in the field. This freed me for full time with the CWCC and the Chinese Social Service office. I had planned a trip by steamer to Ningpo to revisit the girls' orphanage and encourage the Chinese personnel and sisters to continue the hygienic practices my students and I had taught them. I was particularly concerned for the infants, who had been diapered in harsh, faded denim. We had sent the orphanage bales of immaculately white, soft diapers which we found they had not used at all when we visited later. The students told me the Chinese thought Westerners were dirty because we used such clean cloth on that part of the baby's anatomy. There had also been the question of flies drowning in the prepared formula. The orphanage was headed by a European Sister who told me she had difficulty in getting the Chinese staff, lay and religious, to obey orders that contradicted Chinese custom.

Thus it was that I planned this trip for early February and decided to go alone this time without an interpreter.

Before I left, Lucile and I helped with interviews of Shanghai's foreign population anxious to leave China. Quotas had opened up or been increased in many countries, including the USA, Brazil, Canada and the Philippines. The screening may have taken place in a civic building, if not Aurora College, for I remember long tables in large rooms. From ghettos of the city came hundreds of Jews, Eurasians, White Russians, Polish and other refugees. In my interviews with Jews I was indelibly impressed by the diplomas, degrees and honorary documents from leading universities and academies of music and arts laid before me. I discovered then how little I knew about the persecution in Germany. I asked an elderly man if his family was still in the homeland he had left. In the solemn dignity of his dry-eyed gaze and in his very silence I realized I had intruded into the forbidden room of his deepest privacy and sorrow.

Following the week or so of interviews, I was ready to go on my trip. The steamer, scheduled to leave at ten o'clock, still had not moved by early afternoon. I waited impatiently in my cabin, puzzled by the long delay and chafing because I had failed to bring any writing or reading materials.

Before the young steward took my ticket, I had waited on deck but soon chose to make my way to my room and stay there. Not only was the deck crammed with people, a fact I was accustomed to by now, but as I passed through the crowd, all sound of talking stopped. I was used to being the focus of stares, even of amusement due to my strange garb, but in this silence I felt hostility. Finally, a knock on my cabin door promised an explanation of the long delay. However, I found a delegation of two or three young officers in naval uniform. Politely but gravely they summoned me to follow them. As in a dream, I remember the wide flight of stairs leading to a large room below. Around a long table sat other white-uniformed officers. Were they naval or simply the steamer's personnel? I never knew. They looked like Navy to me. I remember being conscious of my waist-length gray veil and my own uniform that is so unlike a nun's habit. I think I probably swished the veil and straightened my shoulders as if being led to execution. When I stood before the unsmiling man at the head of the table, he asked in perfect English for my papers. I produced. After silent perusal, he shared my credentials with the man next to him.

He then asked why I was making this trip. While I explained I sensed that he doubted my word. With all the firmness I could muster I challenged him to confirm my story and call Father McGuire or McGoey, whose names I felt sure were well known to all men of business or commerce in Shanghai. However, he motioned to an aide to see me to the staircase, which I ascended alone and with relief. I was never to know the reason for our ship's delay. My presence may or may not have been the cause. Very soon, whistles blew and we began to move out.

I went to the big dining room at dinnertime and took my place at the huge round table, set for perhaps twenty-five. The moment I entered the room, again all conversation ceased. At the table, no one spoke. A youthful waiter then came to my chair.

"Chinese chow or American chow?" he asked in an arrogant tone. In the best Mandarin I knew, I told him I wanted not only Chinese food but chopsticks. He had placed silverware at my plate. I thought I heard a kind of sigh go around the table. When I took up the chopsticks and maneuvered the first morsels of food to my mouth, everyone relaxed and began to converse. My own neighbor on the right asked in good English what my uniform represented. When I said I was a Catholic sister, she nodded her understanding and immediately passed the word to her other neighbor. I knew I was "in" when smiling diners began to offer me choice portions from the countless dishes, holding them out to me with their own chopsticks.

What any of that—the silences, the interrogation on the lower deck—was about I did not know and never learned.

At the Ningpo orphanage, Sister Superior assured me that the CWCC supplies had arrived and all was in order. She assured me, too, that our suggestions were being followed diligently by kitchen and crêche personnel, so I settled in for a few days of rest and relaxed observation of the needs of the children and clinic.

I had not told the Superior about the hostility I sensed on the trip from Shanghai, nor about the odd interrogation by the naval officers. I had begun to think my feelings were probably paranoid. However, Sister told me that missionaries fleeing from villages in the interior were reporting that Mao was not only winning the war, but winning the people. He had ordered his men to treat peasants with respect and punished any soldier who robbed or molested them. The practical peasants were convinced he intended to keep the promises he made for equal land and raised status. Village by village, he was trying to establish his program and if he could not, due to war, he was establishing himself as a leader in whom to believe, a leader who gave hope. Chiang was giving nothing. Mao was not only outmaneuvering Chiang's army, but soon would outnumber it if Nationalist soldiers continued to defect as they were doing.

—15—

A Change in the Wind

While I was away at Ningpo, the sisters at home in Shanghai attended the first Catholic Conference on Education ever held in that city. Cardinal Tien and Bishop Paul Yu Pin presided.

Before my trip to Ningpo Sister Alice told me it might be my last CWCC visitation. My continued weight loss, blurred vision and deep fatigue disturbed her. On my return, she noticed a jaundiced, yellowish tinge to my complexion, and that settled it. She was delighted that I could type, and my new job would be secretarial in her own office at the convent. That was fine with me, but it was not to be for long.

As spring advanced, Sister Alice showed signs of strain. She had survived the enormous privations, fears and anxieties of the war years only to undertake the responsibilities and stress of starting this new branch of our society. Evidently her letters alerted her Superior to a need for rest. A wire came from Sister Margaret, directing her to take a six-month vacation at Peking (Beijing). Lucile would take over as Acting Superior.

Sister Lucile strongly felt that we needed to enjoy more recreational activities together as a family. Therefore, I recall, we attended a Chinese opera.

We sat on long, backless, wooden benches in a large hall below a slightly raised platform. I remember decorative banners of brilliant reds and yellows on the walls, good lighting for the stage, and exquisitely costumed, black-wigged actors and their traditional, stylized masks. We sat shoulder to shoulder with parents, children and their *amah*s. Everyone was busily eating, shelling peanuts or otherwise munching on goodies, reminiscent of baseball fans back home. A constant parade of vendors made their sales around and over the heads of all. These were followed by boys with buckets of wet towels which they wrung out and tossed to reaching hands. The used towels were then flung back, rinsed and tossed again to others.

One afternoon Sister Lucile and I took in a John Wayne movie, shown in a hall used for meetings, not a theater. Candida was too busy to go with us and seemed uninterested. Magdolna was definitely not interested since her English was unequal to the sound track, and Chinese subtitles would be no help to her. Lucile and I enjoyed the touch of home the movie gave us, and I understood now why my students were so well informed about Western styles in hair-do and dress which they imitated so well. I had heard them mention Olivia de Havilland and other stars. This had to be within the context of only the past year or two, however, unless the Japanese had shown American films during occupation, which I doubt.

We hired a young college student to be our houseboy to help with general maintenance and chores, a tremendous boon. This gave Magdolna time for Mandarin and English lessons. Already the sisters in charge of a hospital in Chengtu had asked for her services, urging her to master enough Chinese to find out where patients hurt, at the very least.

Magdolna seemed more and more at peace as she became involved in her new life in China. When she first arrived she was almost afraid to breathe for fear of germs. With the onset of summer's scorching heat, the government called for cooperation in a massive effort to inoculate every child in Shanghai against cholera. Sister Candida turned her center into a clinic. She obtained the necessary serum and equipment and asked Sister Magdolna to vaccinate the parish children. She did not tell the mothers beforehand, believing they would not come. The day they came for their relief supplies Candida was able to convince them that the shot was necessary protection for their children. I dropped in while Magdolna was jabbing small arms with the needle and I was very impressed by the stoicism of even the smallest child. Maybe a wince, but never a whimper. Through open windows I had heard infants cry for what seemed hours at a time, apparently without any attention. As I watched these toddlers take these shots that make strong men quail, I presumed their training began at birth.

Candida's work flourished. Perhaps the sight of more sisters in gray, even though only five of us, impressed the Catholic Chinese our community was now a solid actuality. The mothers who joined her sewing club in increasing numbers were not of the peasant class but wives of successful merchants. Their fashionable dresses with Mandarin collars distinguished them from working-class women, who customarily wore dark trousers and hip-length jackets. They appreciated the new sister's work with their children, and Candida had enough volunteer help to start a club for teenagers which, of course, she did. The parishioners of all ages loved the idea of a bazaar. They entered into preparations with vigor and imagination, raising considerable funds for Sister's work. (This would be allowed to continue for two years after Mao took over. Then, suddenly, it would be stopped with the closing of churches at the end of 1951.)

All went smoothly under Lucile's strong, experienced direction. She became increasingly involved in teaching and counseling at Aurora, where the School of Social Work attracted more and more students. Her fun-loving disposition, hearty laugh and warm enthusiasm appealed to the young people, who eagerly signed up for her classes.

As for me, without a definite assignment, I was on call to fill in where needed. Sister Lucile took me along on errands or shopping by jeep, and I was able to share much of my thinking with her. Sights and sounds and customs that had lost their novelty for me I enjoyed all over again as I watched her face express amazement, amusement, surprise and, always, rich appreciation of the moment. She was more practical than I, her curiosity was aroused by the "how-to" of everything, from food preparation to all other phases of Chinese daily life.

Now I had time to visit patients in the hospital, referred to me by clergy and other friends. The Daughters of Charity had the only TB hospital ward, and I regularly dropped in to chat with young Michael Lee. He was a graduate of the University of Peking, where he had been converted and baptized by one of the Jesuit priests. Michael lay flat on a cot in a large, airy men's ward.

"I haven't seen the moon in nine years," he told me wistfully. He looked transparently pale and scarcely made a bulge beneath the white bedclothes, yet he always smiled and spoke cheerfully. The only item Michael ever asked me to bring him was the incense we all used to banish mosquitoes. This came in the shape of small cones and was very effective.

After I returned to the States, he sent me one or two poems he had written, which I kept for many years before they were lost during one of my many moves. Michael told me that one of my students, whom I will call Susan, came every Sunday after church and relayed the sermon she had heard to the entire ward. Her audience looked forward to her visits, and I am sure the pretty, vivacious girl brightened their long, uneventful day.

With Magdolna and Lucile I now had time to study Mandarin. American Bishop James Walsh, of Maryknoll, was one of our classmates at Aurora. He treated us like a kindly uncle and we appreciated his interest in our young community. His concern was to be expressed effectively at a time Sister Candida would need it most.

A Change in the Wind

For the first time, I studied the written language and fell in love with it. Here, in each Chinese character, each word picture, I felt I was truly finding the real China, an entity I had sought in landscape, village street, and in the calm, enigmatic faces of the people. But I had known it was not there, not in any external manifestation or hiding place. The real China, I realized, lay in its pervading spirit, even spirituality. This revealed itself in pictograms created by Chinese thought and interpersonal communication centuries before the Christian era.

Learning the characters was for me a long, drawn-out process, for I wanted to linger on each one, meditatively. For example, the simple word for 'good' is the pictogram or picture of a mother and child. The word for 'patience' pictures a heart with a knife or dagger over it, rendering the word 'patience' interchangeable with the concept of endurance and, I understand, tolerance. To be patient is to endure whatever momentary annoyance or suffering, and the same character tells us to be patient with differences of others.

Delighted with the language, I thought I understood at last why "East is East and West is West and never the twain shall meet." The race that would devise a language so graphically interiorized, spiritual in thrust, is feminine, I believe, opposed to the masculinity of many Western languages. And how does the female person get along with the male? It happens, or there would be no marriages. In childhood I had fallen in love with China and all things Chinese through exposure to its arts and artifacts. Now by listening and learning its wisdom, respect, admiration and understanding took root.

–16–

Waning of the Moon

In mid-summer, Chiang Kai-shek called in all foreign and Chinese national currency. CNC had escalated to sixteen million to one U.S. dollar and every household must have possessed baskets full of paper money. All of it was worthless overnight. Instead, the government issued GPY, the gold yuan, at four to one dollar. No one liked it. No one knew how to deal with it. Anyone caught dealing in the black market would be shot.

The first to be shot was a fifteen-year-old boy. This sickened me. Up to this time I had been neutral toward Chiang Kai-shek—but no more. The parades to the execution ground became daily events, raucous celebrations, enforced, ominous and terrifying.

Hunger set in. We saw angry men and women outside grocery stores, whose owners refused to open shop. People held fistfuls of CNC above their heads to show they had the money to pay. But grocers didn't want the money that in two days' time or less would be useless to them. I saw sacks of rice dumped into the gutter by angry coolies, who raided the store when they could not buy food. The blazing hatred in the eyes and faces of these marauders, combined with a new arrogance, was frightening. Undoubtedly, they had direct news of the war. They would have learned the Communist forces, two million strong, now matched Chiang's army. Nationalist forces were on the run. The laboring class, believing in Mao Tse Tung, had given its heart to him, and their arrogance that I noted was the expression of confidence in his victory.

The CWCC fathers shared supplies of canned goods with all the mission houses in Shanghai, so we did not experience actual hunger. But we lacked the vitamins and balanced diet needed for healthy eyes and teeth.

The spring and summer months of 1948 were all I would have of the China experience. My own health deteriorated, still undiagnosed, and Dr. Alice Pan recommended my return to the States for more complete tests, not available in Shanghai. Sister Lucile notified Sister Frederica and soon I was summoned home.

When my ticket had been purchased and the date of my leaving set, many of my former students came with gifts to say farewell. Rowena, dear to me as a daughter by now, gave me a rosewood fan that I treasured for memories it brought of her faithful devotion. Another gift I loved and wore during the weeks ahead of convalescence in the States was a pongee silk kimono with blue and green embroidered butterflies, from Marie, my companion and interpreter on jeep trips to the orphanages. These young women and their social work classmates had shown a courage, strength of will and aggressive assertiveness I had never suspected in the Chinese female character. I found them daring, humorous, ready for all that our modern age could and would offer them, whether in ideas or in action. I had certainly seen all of this in Candida and in our society's other Chinese member, Sister Malia, who came to our community in Los Angeles already a graduate in engineering.

The sisters drove me to the airport next day. We chattered inconsequentially, as one does at such times, promising to write, to pray for each other. I waved from the window as the enormous Pan Am bird taxied away. When it began the ascent, I saw my China slipping away beneath me, and I wept.

When the tears stopped spilling, I stared out over the ocean and gradually, lazily, not pushing for thoughts, began to sort out my nearly two years of "wind and moon." What had I learned and what impressions would I carry like tattoos on my memory?

I had gone to China with my heart in my hands, overeager to love and be loved by the Chinese people. But I learned very soon that my approach was naive, childish, based on sincere goodwill but rooted in ignorance of the Chinese mind. I found my enthusiasm for all that was Chinese met with very cool, polite, smiling rebuff. Nothing overt or expressed. Just an impenetrable wall of otherness, a wall as palpable as a picket sign declaring me forever a foreigner, an outsider. Even Candida, my own close associate in this venture, seemed to retreat behind this wall as soon as we landed on China's soil. So, I might conclude, in these few months I had begun at thirty-six to grow up.

I had had a childhood fascination with San Francisco's Chinatown and the enchanting stores full of tiny, tinkly ornamental wares, fragrant incense, the total otherness of Oriental imagination and art. I never lost the fascination, and indeed sailed for China with the feeling I was going home. All that Chinatown gave me in childhood seemed exactly right for me. Therefore, I must have presumed that the Chinese would realize this at once and take me to their hearts. Not at all. Now I know they are amused by our fascination with the Oriental culture and its artistic expressions. They know in their wisdom that they are not as fragile as the ornaments that we admire. They identify with the wisdom and depth of their ancient, great philosophers. We will never understand nor meet them heart to heart until we discover that depth which is their truth. And we may never do so in this world. It will be enough, however, if we respect them, knowing it is there.

From the Russians, on the other hand, whom I had stereotyped unconsciously and, no doubt, consciously too, I found immediate acceptance as strong as an embrace. Warmth, humor and loving kindness sang out from the

Russian character as I experienced it in the White Russian women who worked with me and the Ukrainian men who labored at hauling UNRRA goods. In that experience I learned how much we impoverish ourselves mentally and spiritually by not reaching out to understand, know and become acquainted with our fellow human beings whatever their culture and wherever on earth they live.

As soon as Candida and I were again peers in the give and take of the larger community, our relationship resumed its original state of pleasant, casual ease. During the months that I was acting head of our tiny embryonic branch of the SSS, she did not accept me in my appointed position. Decisions were reached, of course, in mutual agreement, but the responsibility was mine in the end. However, this was not the USA but China, Candida's territory. I had backed off, leaving her complete freedom in the work for which she was trained and experienced. In household matters, we usually agreed because we carried on our routines of community prayer and chores just as we had at home. So we got along, waiting for the others to join us, going our individual ways, yet missing the community life that was family to both of us and which we could not seem to achieve together. From this situation I became aware that all the orphanages were headed by a single European nun with many Chinese under her direction. I began to think that Candida may have been keenly conscious that we were peers in age and training. Why was she, the Chinese sister, not chosen to be acting Superior instead of the American? I do not think she really thought this. But she well might have felt it. Sister Alice's seniority in age and experience, on the other hand, made her selection obvious to head our foundation. Still, I hoped the day would come when our society would let its branches be headed by a native of the country it served. (This is now true.)

What friends had I made in China? Through Candida and her family I had met many men and women of the educated and wealthy class. We had been entertained in the home of Dr. John C. Wu, an eminent Catholic layman, who was a scholar, author and philosopher. We had been honored to be the only guests in his home that evening. But though we met and were hosted by many Chinese men and women of the elite, we had no close friendships or association with them. That was normally so, for in the USA or any country a religious community is an object of interest for its dedication and humanitarian service rather than for the personality of its members. It was among the young people with whom we worked or taught, with whom we had daily meaningful contact, that we formed lasting friendships.

However, I count foremost among my friendships in Shanghai the spiritual guide I met soon after arrival in 1946. This was a Hungarian priest, a newly ordained Jesuit in his early thirties named Father Lazslo Ladanyi. He had a deeply contemplative nature and was totally in love with China and its people. He had been teaching at Peking University and was spending a year in Shanghai, fulfilling a requirement of his Jesuit order toward completion of his spiritual formation. He became my mentor and opened my mind to a depth of China's beauty I might not have recognized. To compare Western youth to Eastern, he once told me that a Western youth might stand on a little bridge over a running stream and point out a dozen attractive objects. He would name the birds flying above, comment on the flora and fauna. In short, the Western mind revels in recognition and tabulation of what the eye sees. The Eastern youth, on the other hand, would lean over the railing of the bridge and gaze into the stream for a long time, saying nothing. He would be experiencing the stream, feeling the flora and fauna in his soul. The Western mind reaches out to know the outer garment rather than the inner essence, so attractive to the Eastern.

In my travels by jeep, I often saw little arches, like gate-

Waning of the Moon

ways to houses no longer there. Father Ladanyi told me there were never any houses to these gates. The whole purpose of the arch was to frame a particular view pleasing to the builder.

"Stand and look through the next archway," he told me, "and view the picture that is framed this way."

I came to understand these little oddities of the Chinese point of view as the delicacy of appreciative thought.

From Candida I had learned bits of information concerning opinions Chinese held regarding nationalities with commercial or other influence in China. The Germans, she said, were most respected. Russians were not liked or respected because of weakness for drink. The Chinese do not have this weakness. Theirs is gambling. The British were not high on the scale of esteem, nor the French. We, the Americans, were congratulated for achievement and material success. Liked? I didn't get the impression we were. I learned that of the three Soong sisters, all of whom had married government leaders, one loved power (Madame Chiang), one loved money (wife of the finance minister) and one loved China (a Communist, widow of Sun Yat Sen.)

To end my reverie, as well as this memoir, I searched my prayerbook for a holy card given to me by Father Ladanyi. The front showed a Chinese Virgin Mary kneeling before a Chinese Angel Gabriel, announcing that she was to become the mother of the Savior. On the back Father Ladanyi had spontaneously penned the following lines, searching his English vocabulary to interpret his Hungarian thoughts. He had then handed the poem to me, and I knew it was a lesson in what it meant to be a missionary.

Lord,
*I have not come to conquer
but to serve, like Mary;
You called me to leave my country,
to see the work of the Spirit
through thousands of eyes in China;
to admire her beauty, her spiritual depth,
and to find Your suffering Face
in her daily life;
to fall in love with this country You gave me
to build Your kingdom here.*

—17—

What Happened After

Soon after my departure, Sister Alice returned from Peking. Her first concern was to find the community a larger house in order to accommodate new members. By Christmas they had moved to a suitable location near Christ the King Church and received two young ladies as aspirants.

By now the old China was crumbling and the new was a threatening force. Sister Frederica, alarmed by reports that Chiang's government had fled to Taiwan, reached the Sisters by phone. She urged them to come home as soon as possible. Magdolna returned to Shanghai from Chengtu. The first to fly home was Lucile. Alice, a Hungarian, obtained a visa through the Vatican Legation at Nanking. Magdolna, also Hungarian, was denied. She and Candida remained alone until August, when she gained passage on a Canada-bound repatriation ship.

Candida carried on her parish work until Christmas 1951, when churches were closed. She was then joined by Sister Malia Rosa, who had been in the novitiate when Candida and I left for China. She was now a professed sister, with a master's in social work. She chose to return to China, fearing reprisals on her family. (Arrested in 1962 as a spy and sentenced to seven years in prison, Sister Malia Rosa died in solitary confinement in 1969.)

Whereas I returned to the comforts of my own culture and the care of my religious family, Candida would spend eight harrowing years of political harassment, serious illnesses, economic hardship, house arrest and repeated interrogations. In 1957, she was granted permission to leave during a slight relaxation of the Communist clamp-down on exit visas. After six months with her family in Hong Kong, she flew home at last to the motherhouse in Los Angeles.

To Sister Candida belongs credit for the dream come true. Hers was the vision of a Chinese branch of the society. In 1963 Sisters Candida, Pauline, Angelia, and Ancilla, M.D., all Chinese, along with one American sister, founded the branch in Taipei, Taiwan.

Candida retired after fifteen years' service in Taipei. After a long and debilitating illness, she died in 1981. According to the sisters who cared for Candida, "her greatest gift was her ability to touch lives and speak a language of the heart that called a marvelous variety of people to love her. She was, and continues to be, a real force in our lives."

Appendix: An Historical Perspective

A brief survey of the major political events occurring in China during the times described in this book.

1945
THE EMERGENCE OF MAO TSE-TUNG AND THE CULT OF MAO

The Seventh Congress of the Chinese Communist Party (CCP) met in Yenan and was in session from April 23–June 11, 1945 (the first Party Congress since the Sixth, in Moscow, in 1928). At this time there were 1.2 million party members and of this number no more than 1,000 remained from those who had joined before 1927, and no more than 20,000 from those who had joined between 1927 and 1937.

CCP celebrated the Seventh Congress as one of "solidarity and victory." The most important items covered were Chu Teh's report on military matters, Liu Shao-Chi's report on the revised Constitution, and Mao Tse-tung's celebrated speech on "coalition government."

Mao's speech was a proposal for a "democratic coalition government" in which Communists would be the leaders. It would be "an alliance based on the overwhelming majority of people, under the leadership of the working class." Moreover, he made it very clear that:

"We Communists do not conceal our political views. Definitely, and beyond all doubt, our future or maximum programme is to carry China forward to socialism and communism. Both the name of our party and our Marxist world outlook unequivocally point to this supreme ideal of the future of incomparable brightness and splendor."[1]

Elsewhere in his speech Mao referred to foreign culture, saying, "It would be a wrong policy to shut it out; rather we should as far as possible draw on what is progressive in it for use in the development of China's new culture; it would also be wrong to copy it blindly; rather we should draw on it critically to meet the actual needs of the Chinese people." He applied the same reasoning to China's traditional culture—selectivity for what he saw as China's present and future needs.

Mao also gave the concluding address to the congress on June 11, 1945. In this speech he used the old Chinese fable entitled "The Foolish Old Man Who Removed the Mountains." This fable tells of an old man who had two mountain peaks, Taihang and Wangwo, that obstructed the way in front of his house. He called his sons, and hoe in hand they began to dig up the mountains. Another old man saw them and said, "How silly of you to do this. It is quite impossible for you to dig up these huge mountains." The foolish old man replied, "When I die, my sons will carry on; when they die, there will be my grandsons, and their sons and grandsons, and so on to infinity. High as the mountains are, they cannot grow any higher, and with every bit we dig they will be that much lower. Why can't we clear them away?" With that, the old man went on digging every day, unshaken in his conviction. God was moved by this and sent down two angels who carried the mountains away on their backs.

Mao cited the immediate relevance of this fable for China's situation: "Today two big mountains lie like a dead weight on China's people. One is imperialism and the other is feudalism. The Chinese Communist Party has long made up its mind to dig them out. We must persevere and work unceasingly, and we, too, will touch God's heart. Our God is none other than the masses of Chinese people. If they stand up and dig together with us, why can't these two mountains be cleared away?"

Mao emerged bigger than life from the Seventh Congress. Both he and his policies were extolled with enormous enthusiasm, and many of his policies were incorporated into the new constitution as "Thought of Mao Tse-tung." CCP, in effect, unified under him at this conference and his victory was translated into power. In short, he had the mandate of heaven!

At the First Plenum of the Seventh Congress the Central Committee elected Mao Tse-tung to the Politburo along with Chu Teh and Chou En-lai and other party notables. Mao was now Chairman of the Central Committee, the Politburo, and the Secretariat. He held the first two chairmanships until he died in 1976. The cult of Mao was well established by the end of the Seventh Congress and it grew, for the most part, until his death.

Japan surrendered August 8, 1945, barely two months after the Seventh Congress ended. The question then for China was—could a "democratic coalition government" work? Party goals were different and the Soviet Union was playing an ambivalent role. Stalin did not think the Communists could win a war against the Nationalist government, or Kuomintang (KMT), and wasn't sure he wanted them to. For one reason, he thought Mao leaned more toward national socialism than toward international socialism. In other words, he wasn't sure Mao would recognize the USSR as the mother of international socialism/communism and knuckle under. For another reason, he didn't think CCP could win, and he did not want to come out on the losing side. So he backed Chiang Kai-shek and signed a Treaty of Friendship with KMT on August 14, 1945, less than a week after Japan surrendered. On the other hand, Stalin did give help to the Communists in Manchuria. The evidence is still out as to how much help he gave, but he did give some direct economic, political and military aid to CCP. A few historians (mostly Russians) believe "the amount of help given was sufficient to play a determinative role in the concluding phase of the Chinese people's liberation struggle."[2] In any case, when Japan surrendered each side had advantages:

The Communists were situated in northern China as a result of penetration and work during the war and following their offensive during the summer of 1945. This was somewhat neutralized by MacArthur's warning to Japan of the importance of surrendering only to the Nationalists. The Communists were well disciplined, unified and obedient to high-level orders. They had a goal, knew where they were going, and believed mightily in their cause. One disadvantage was that although they wanted Soviet help, they did not want to do anything that would subordinate them to the Soviet Union.

The Nationalists were recognized as the legal government of China, and China was considered one of the Big Five world powers. Chiang Kai-shek enjoyed the highest degree of national popularity in the relieved atmosphere of Japan's defeat. He had the support of the U.S., who not least of all transported approximately 500,000 Nationalist soldiers to the northern and eastern part of the country where they were able to disarm 1.25 million Japanese troops. They had superiority in conventional war capability and 3 to 1 superiority in fighting men (5 to 1 in terms of men in arms). They had a monopoly in air and naval units, and tremendous superiority in firepower. They also had the Sino-Soviet Friendship Treaty of August 14, 1945.

KMT's disadvantage was that it was weary of war, divided into factions, mired in corruption, weak in fighting strategy and couldn't get its act together.

CCP's leaders were divided at war's end as to how to deal with the Nationalists. Caught up in the ambivalence (contradiction) implicit in Mao's "democratic coalition government" speech to the Seventh Congress, some were disposed to talk rather than fight. However, Mao, believing absolutely in the ultimate victory, saw in this ambivalence the opportunity to continue to build and train their/his military strength to that end during the peace negotiations. This was part of his zig-zag method of operation—you go there in order to get here. Put the spotlight there in order to better your position here. No matter what was involved, to Mao it was legitimate strategy.

Following this line of reasoning, on August 24, 1945, CCP accepted KMT's third invitation to reopen negotiations. Mao and Chou En-lai flew to Chungking August 28, along with Ambassador Patrick Hurley. At the opening banquet Mao surprised everyone by his toast to Chiang's long life.

The negotiations lasted for six weeks. The main topics discussed were (1) the "nationalization" of armies, (2) political representation, (3) the method of selecting local officials and (4) the disposition of CCP's base areas. CCP made concessions. In one, they agreed to withdraw from certain base areas. This was a shrewd (zig-zag) move on Mao's part because by withdrawing from some he was able to expand while no one was looking and strengthen his position in others—namely northern China. As a result, by the end of 1945 CCP had basically withdrawn from south China, with the exception of some guerrilla units left behind. Its forces were concentrated well to the north of the Yangtze River. As a result of this basic reshaping of its territory, CCP could now claim control of approximately 150 million people in about a quarter of the most populous area in China.

The negotiations ended October 10, 1945, with an agreement that included these provisions: the convening of a Political Consultative Conference (PCC) that would represent all groups to discuss the democratic reorganization of government and to approve a new constitution. It would create a committee of three composed of a Nationalist, a Communist, and an American to supervise the military reorganization. Mao returned to Yenan (his capital from 1937–47) and Chou En-lai stayed to deal with the details.

The details, however, proved impossible to settle. CCP would not give up the right to appoint officials in its own base areas. This refusal led to the breakdown of the whole conference, and Ambassador Hurley resigned on November 26, 1945, blaming American foreign service officers for undermining his policy (John Service was his main target).

On November 27, President Truman appointed General George Marshall as his special representative to China. (Leighton Stuart took the post of ambassador in July of 1946.)

Mao and CCP showed a new interest in negotiations very quickly, for Moscow had concluded an agreement with KMT on November 27 that removed CCP from the cities of Manchuria. The Communists welcomed General Marshall and agreed to participate in PCC and meet in January 1946.

President Truman on December 15, 1945, called for a "strong, united, democratic China." Mao took this as indication of support for a strong coalition government. Chou En-lai proposed a cease-fire during the PCC meetings, and with Marshall's help this was agreed to. With the exceptions of the areas south of the Yangtze River and in Manchuria, all troop movements were to stop after January 13, 1946.

1946

During 1946 relationships hardened between KMT and CCP. During the January 1946 meetings of PCC (People's Consultative Conference) it was agreed that a National Assembly would be called in May and that local officials, in-

Appendix

cluding governors, would be popularly elected.

In February the Committee of Three (one KMT, one Communist, and one American) reached an agreement to reorganize the military in a way that would still ensure KMT its five-to-one ratio of superiority. But neither CCP nor KMT seemed to understand or accept what "coalition" really meant, and as a result the terms of the February agreement broke down. By May, however, things had shifted in Manchuria and when KMT was able to occupy Changchun and when Marshall began to pressure both sides to get together and negotiate, KMT agreed to a two-week cease fire on May 24, 1946, which was subsequently extended until the end of June. But both sides hardened and by the end of June it was obvious that the final test of power was about to begin. KMT was anxious to press its military advantage, and CCP had succeeded in buying enough time to regroup, consolidate and expand. They were able to make it appear that KMT was responsible for the resort to a military solution. But whatever Mao's thinking was, CCP had never really relied on the success of negotiations and he felt he couldn't rely on either Russian or American help. By this time, however, it didn't matter because Mao's program of self-reliance had become his main weapon. In addition, through Party education, including land reform, he had succeeded in gaining the backing of the peasants, particularly the poor and landless who made up about 70 percent of the rural population in the Liberated Areas. In the eyes of some historians, this consolidation of social and political support for the Communist-led government constituted probably the most important single factor in the making of CCP.

Civil war began again in earnest in the summer of 1946. By late June KMT armies began the offensive in the Central Plains. In July there was more fighting in Shantung (Shantong) and in Kiangsu (Jiangsu). The civil war was fought in three stages as Mao saw it.

The first of these was the period from July, 1946 to June, 1947—the *defensive stage*. During this time KMT was in the ascendancy and CCP took the brunt, allowing KMT to penetrate deeply into North China. Mao used the method of strategic withdrawal and mobile warfare, abandoning the cities and towns for the countryside. Lin Biao's troops moved north of the Sungari River, leaving the rest of Manchuria to the Nationalists. Li, another general, moved out of central China into Shansi (Shanxi). CCP consolidated and tightened up within their areas of strength and otherwise fought a war of attrition.

KMT reached its peak in March of 1947 with its capture of Yenan (Ya'nan), which CCP ceded without contest. Mao himself went into the backcountry of Shansi.

1947

The second stage of the civil war began in 1947. This is called the stage of *limited counteroffensive*. CCP continued to rely on mobile warfare. They eroded the strength of the Nationalist forces while at the same time extending the range of engagements. Chiang Kai-shek overextended himself fatally by sending most of his best troops into important but remote Manchuria. Mao's main objective at this point was to direct the counteroffensive against the "soft underbelly" of central China and at the major north-south railways that moved through north China.

By the end of 1947 the Communists were able to cut the railway lines both north and south of Mukden (Shenyang) and to take Shejiazhuang in Hebei. This linked together the two base areas that lay in the path of the strategic Beijing-Hankow railway.

On December 25, 1947, Mao gave a well-publicized explanation of the Communist war strategy. He listed ten principles of operation for the coming counteroffensive. The main ones were:

Appendix

¶ The prime objective was to eliminate the strength of KMT rather than acquire land or towns.

¶ The People's Liberation Army (PLA) would operate against enemy units that were dispersed and isolated, and this would continue until the balance of forces began to swing to the Communist side.

¶ PLA would hold off on attacks on enemy towns and large concentrations.

¶ Battles of attrition that might end in equal losses would be avoided.

¶ PLA would attack only when numerically superior forces could be brought to bear.

¶ The main source of supply of both arms and personnel was to come from the enemy.

In addition to these war strategy principles, Mao enumerated and employed other tactics and programs aimed at gaining popular support:

¶ He emphasized positive and effective programs which CCP would put into use to show they meant business.

¶ If the programs resulted in mistakes, Mao said they could learn from the mistakes and adjust programs accordingly.

¶ The principal program that the Communists used most effectively was land reform. Mao's ultimate vision was that there would be no private land ownership, but reasoned that he would have to move toward this goal in several steps.

Land reform had immediate and profound appeal to millions of destitute peasants. The promise of a fair share of land was enough to mobilize most of the volunteer soldiers necessary to win the war. However, coercive methods were also used.

The Communists carried out an experimental phase of land reform between May 4, 1946, and October 10, 1947. The lessons learned during this phase were discussed at the National Land Conference held in a village of Hebei in

September of 1947, with about 1,000 delegates attending. The conference passed an Outline Land Law which was published October 10. It became the basic text for similar meetings throughout the liberated (Communist) areas. The document stated that China's land conditions were the root of its "being the victim of aggression, poverty, backwardness and the basic obstacle to our country's democratization, industrialization, independence, unity, strength and prosperity." This put the focus directly on the gentry class. The new law was radical and systematic. Its target was to get rid of the landlord class, as a class, and to equalize land ownership. It was a throwback to Sun Yat-sen's "land to the tiller" idea. The program was administered by various village associations. Idealistic as the program was, it was too full of contradictions and errors to work. Its immediate failure probably came because it hit the middle peasants too hard and the overall countryside was too poor (landwise and otherwise) to make the equalization of wealth possible. In other words, as wealthy as some landlords and rich peasants might have been, their redistributed properties wouldn't have been enough to make the destitute rural population into middle-class peasants.

1948

In January of 1948 Mao defined the difference between middle and rich peasants. A middle peasant was one who derived no more than 25 percent of his income from the exploitation of the labor of others, while rich peasants exceeded this.[3]

As a result of the new land policy violence increased. Mao felt that some violence was useful but that excessive violence could not be permitted to impede the developing military situation. Mao also insisted that different types of areas be discriminated, and that appropriate policies be used in each area:

¶ "Old Liberated Areas," those areas that had been under control since 1945, required only minor adjustments of land conditions.

¶ The "semi-old areas," those areas occupied between 1945 and mid-1947, had special problems. The middle peasants had a wait-and-see attitude, while the poor peasants were in a demanding mood. Poor peasants' leagues were to be organized to deal with the situation. More violence was to be expected in these areas.

¶ The "new liberated areas," those areas taken since mid-1947, were to experience land reform only in stages.

¶ The remaining areas, the "guerrilla zone," adjoined enemy territory and the new liberated areas. Here, in order to curtail violence, reform had to be confined to propaganda, covert organized work, and the distribution of certain movable property. Massive organized work could not be organized openly, nor could reforms be implemented in these marginal areas.

During the winter of 1947-48, Mao took advantage of the improving war situation to conduct a new rectification campaign. He felt this campaign was necessary in order to deal with errors and contradictions in the massive, complicated land reform program. There were other reasons for it also. The most urgent, he felt, was that CCP had grown from 1.2 million members in April 1945 to 2.7 million by mid-1947. This increase in number had allowed many "landlords, rich peasants and riff-raff...to sneak into CCP."[4] Mao believed that these elements "did control a number of Party government and peoples' organizations, tyrannically abuse their power, ride roughshod over other people, distort the Party's policies and thus alienate these organizations from the masses."[5] This campaign (*zheng feng*) sought to educate those who could be redeemed and to reject those who could not. The campaign was different from earlier rectification campaigns in that for the first time it invited criticism from non-Party individuals as well as Party members.

In early 1948 a similar program was conducted in the PLA. Here the objectives were on greater political unity, improved living conditions, and the learning of better military techniques.

For the most part this rectification program was suspended in 1948 as Mao turned his attention to the final military showdown.

The third and final stage of the civil war began in the late summer of 1948. PLA numbered over 2 million men and for the first time reached parity with Chiang's army. KMT by mid-1948 was clearly on the defensive. About 300,000 of its troops were isolated in Manchuria and another 100,000 were tied down at Jinanin Shandong. Cities behind Nationalist lines were inundated with inflation and morale was ebbing. Political unrest and turmoil flared up in Nanking (Nanjing).

CCP made the most of KMT's weakened position by launching an all-out strategic offensive. Within five months in the fall and winter of 1948–49, in four major campaigns the Communists broke the back of KMT's army:

In the *first campaign* Jinan (Shandong) was captured on September 24, 1948. Chiang, against advice to the contrary, insisted upon defending it. He lost 100,000 men and 50,000 rifles, mostly, it is said, from psychological rather than military reasons.[6]

The *second campaign* had to do with Lin Biao's Northeast Field Army in Manchuria. His army was now twice the size of Chiang's army in Manchuria. He moved onto the offensive and captured Jinzhow, an important junction and supply base, in mid-October 1948. This destroyed KMT's communication system and disoriented the Nationalist army. Changchun fell on October 19, and Mukden (Shenyang) on November 2. By this time KMT troops were defecting by the droves, and the few remaining positions quickly gave in.

Appendix

1949

The *third campaign*, the Hwai-Hai, lasted from November 6, 1948, to January 10, 1949. It is referred to as Chiang Kai-shek's Waterloo. Here about 600,000 men of the east China and central plains field armies (Communists) surrounded about the same number of Nationalist soldiers in a wide area north of the Hwai (Yellow) River around the city of Xuzhow. Despite good air support, the Nationalists were beaten, as the Communists tightened in on the siege. The Communists were now cleared to the Yangtze River.

The *fourth and last campaign* was in the Peking-Tianjin area. Tianjin surrendered on January 15, 1949. One week later, Fu Zuoyi, the KMT general who had been secretly negotiating with the Communists, turned Peking over to Lin Biao. Over half a million men were lost to the Nationalists in this campaign, and a pattern was established for other KMT generals to follow in turning cities over to the Communists. Peking became the new capital of the Communist government, and by March, 1949, the new administration moved in.

The Second Plenum of the Seventh Congress was held in Hebei, March 5 to 13, 1949. Mao looked to the period ahead and to the establishment of a firm United Front policy that would include democrats who were not party members. Accordingly, the plenum approved the establishment of a new Chinese Peoples' Consultative Conference (CPCC) and the establishment of a democratic coalition government.

At the plenum, Mao cautioned his jubilant followers: "To win the countryside victory is only the first step in a long march of 10,000 *li*." Apparently Mao's caution came from realization that CCP's center of gravity had now shifted from the villages to the city, and he knew that rural ways of life were not city ways of life. He realized the cadres were not prepared for city ways and they would have trouble adjusting. He warned them that party life in the cities would be different from the villages. He told them they would have to change their rural habits and guerrilla mentality. In the rural areas of north China the gentry class and rich peasants had largely been dispossessed and removed from real power. But in the cities, capitalists were still needed for economic reconstruction and development, so they must be protected from the more radically oriented workers; and this Mao was determined to do, at least through the democracy period. So as urban policy developed from 1947 to 1949, CCP became more conservative and leftist excesses were corrected. Meanwhile, in the countryside the job of the cadres was to step up agricultural production. Mao made it clear that the countryside should produce enough to feed itself *and* the cities, *and* have enough left over to export in order to buy needed equipment and technology abroad.

In early 1949, Chiang Kai-shek resigned as President of KMT. He was succeeded by acting President Li Zongren. Li sent a delegation to Peking, but the talks broke down on April 2, 1949 when the Nationalists rejected the Communists' ultimatum. By April 21, the Second and Third Field Armies of PLA began moving across the Yangtze River. The Nationalists were so demoralized by that time that they offered little resistance. The Communist army swept the Yangtze River Valley: Nanking (Nanjing) fell on April 23, Hankou (Hangzhow) on May 3, Wuhan on May 17, and Shanghai on May 27. Lanchou in Gansu was captured August 26, and the other northwestern provinces soon surrendered. In August, CCP started a new offensive in south China, and the whole southeastern littoral was taken by fall. The western provinces of Guizhow, Sichuan, Yunnan and Xikang fell by December of 1949.

1950

In April of 1950, Hainan Island was captured. Tibet fell

Appendix

in late 1950. Only Taiwan escaped capture, and it became the home of what was left of the Nationalist government and its military, about two million strong.

American Ambassador Stuart remained in Nanking. The Communist leaders who had permitted the abuse of American consular officials (and other Americans) in Mukden and elsewhere did invite Stuart on May 13 to visit Mao and Chou En-lai in Peking to discuss U.S.–China relations, but Stuart's authorization did not arrive from Washington until July 2. By then Mao had already announced his "lean to one side" policy and he leaned toward Russia. This policy represented a strong leaning toward Marxist-Leninism regardless of the Soviets' treatment of China during the 1945–49 civil war. This decision cut off the U.S. from China, economically, politically and every other way, and the U.S. became the "enemy" to be vilified in every way possible. This was really nothing new. It had been smoldering since 1945 at least. As long as there might be hope that the U.S. would help CCP on its course, it did not surface with the intensity until KMT was beaten.

Anti-U.S. intensity increased after President Truman put the 7th Fleet in the Taiwan Straits to protect the Nationalists (and Taiwanese) on Taiwan. After that, and the Korean war, the "Hate America" campaigns were stepped up.

Notes

1. Mao Tse-tung, *Selected Works*, Vol. 3, pp. 205–270.
2. O. Borisov, *The Soviet Union and the Manchuria Revolutionary Base*. Moscow Progress Publishers, 1977, p. 46.
3. Mao, "On Some Important Problems of the Party's Present Policy," *Selected Works*, Vol. 4, p. 183.
4. Mao, "On the People's Democratic Dictatorship," *Selected Works*, Vol. 4, p. 415.
5. Ibid.
6. Testimony of the U.S. Consul General at Cingtao. Stuart, *U.S. Relations with China, 1944–9, pp. 330–31*